Two Friends and a Polar Bear

Terry (right) and Aaron enjoying comfort at JFK airport
on their way to Greenland.

Two Friends and a Polar Bear

A Story of Friendship and Endurance Skiing
Unsupported Across the Arctic Greenland Ice Cap

BY

TERRY M. WILLIAMS, M.D.

AND

AARON LINSDAU

Sastrugi Press

Jackson, WY

Sastrugi Press / Published by arrangement with the author

Sastrugi Press: PO Box 1297, Jackson, WY 83001
www.sastrugipress.com

Two Friends and a Polar Bear: A Story of Friendship and Endurance Skiing Unsupported Across the Arctic Greenland Ice Cap

The author has made every effort to accurately recreate conversations, events, and locales from his memories of them. To maintain anonymity, some names and details such as places of residence, physical characteristics, and occupations have been changed. The activities described in this book are inherently dangerous. The publisher does not have any control over and does not assume any responsibility for author or third-party websites or their content.

Any person participating in the activities described in this work is personally responsible for learning the proper techniques and using good judgment. You are responsible for your own actions and decisions. The information contained in this work is subjective and based solely on opinions. No book can advise you to the hazards or anticipate the limitations of any reader. Participation in the described activities can result in severe injury or death. Neither the publisher nor the author assumes any liability for anyone participating in the activities described in this work.

CIP Available
Williams, Terry
Two Friends and a Polar Bear - 1st U.S. ed.
Summary: This story of friendship is about two old friends who plan to ski across the Greenland Icecap along the Arctic Circle in hopes of becoming one of the oldest teams to succeed.

ISBN-13: 978-1-64922-289-3 (paperback)
ISBN-13: 978-1-64922-291-6 (hardback)

910.4

10 9 8 7 6 5

To Diane, the love of my life.

Terry (left) and Aaron enjoying the cold at Camp 9,
a mere 66 miles into their journey.

Table of Contents

"People travel to wonder at the height of the mountains, at the huge waves of the seas, at the long course of the rivers, at the vast compass of the ocean, at the circular motion of the stars, and yet they pass by themselves without wondering."
—St. Augustine, 354–430 A.D.

"Nature is the living, visible garment of God."
—Johann Wolfgang von Goethe

"One touch of nature makes the whole world kin."
—William Shakespeare

"Ye stars, that are the poetry of heaven!"
—Lord Byron

"In her starry shade of dim and solitary loveliness, I learn the language of another world."
—Lord Byron

"For my part, I travel not to go anywhere, but to go. I travel for travel's sake. The great affair is to move; to feel the needs and hitches of our life more nearly; to come down off this feather bed of civilization, and find the globe granite underfoot and strewn with cutting flints. Alas, as we get up in life, and are more preoccupied with our affairs, even a holiday is a thing that must be worked for. To hold a pack upon a pack-saddle against a gale out of the freezing north is no high industry, but it is one that serves to occupy and compose the mind. And when the present is so exacting, who can annoy himself about the future?"
-Robert Louis Stevenson, *Travels with a Donkey in the Cévennes*

Wisdom of Famous Polar Explorers

"There can be little question, therefore, that polar sledging ranks as an easy first as a hunger-producing employment.
—**Robert Falcon Scott**

"It is better to go skiing and think of God, than to go to church and think of sport."
—**Fridtjof Nansen**

"I have often marveled at the thin line which separates success from failure."
Ernest Shackleton

"Adventure is just bad planning."
Roald Amundsen

Terry at Camp 16.

Camp 16: Disappointment

Position: N66° 20.044' W43° 35.791'
Elevation: 8,222'
10.6 miles from Camp 15
Total distance logged between camps: 132.9 miles
Distance to DYE-2: 75.7 miles
Distance to Hill 660: 184 miles

Can we make it? The mileages are daunting. We have used up nearly half of our allotted time, yet we aren't even close to halfway across this endless sea of ice that makes up the Greenland ice cap. We are skiing east to west at roughly the Arctic Circle, crossing the ice cap. Our starting point was at 3,000 feet elevation. Now, we were near this high point at the summit of the ice cap.

Now that we are near the summit, any changes in the terrain are nearly imperceptible—just the changes in the ice and snow surface under our skis are what we notice. The surface will change from wind slab to sastrugi to wind-deposited snow that is soft and unconsolidated. Aaron proclaims this "Greenland National Tarpit Day" because we have been slogging uphill all day through sticky snow that saps our flagging energy levels.

We had a moderate wind all night and woke to a cold morning, maybe -10°F with light snowfall. As usual, we woke at 3 a.m. and started the long slow process of getting ready for a full day of skiing. Everything takes longer in the cold, but at least there is enough twilight this time of year that we don't need our headlamps.

We begin by dressing inside our sleeping bags to preserve our warmth, pulling on down jackets and balaclavas as quickly as we can. Once we are protected from the cold, we exit our warm sleeping bags and re-configure our foam mats to sit on for a quick breakfast.

Yesterday afternoon's chores included melting enough snow for my drinking water today and filling a thermos with hot water for this morning's breakfast. We pass the thermos back and forth to add hot water to our breakfast cereal and coffee mugs and eat in silence. It's tough to carry on much of a conversation with the wind noise on the tent and our down parka hoods pulled up for warmth.

After eating and rinsing our bowls and mugs, and stowing that gear, it's time for final preparations to leave the tent and begin our long day of skiing. We stuff our sleeping bags in their compression sacks. I change from my down booties into my ski boots, while Aaron moves into the vestibule to relieve himself. Once he is done, it's my turn at toilet duties. After filling the scat hole with snow and packing it down, I go back into the tent for the last time this morning.

Meanwhile, Aaron puts his ski boots and gaiters on. We both take our warm down parkas off and begin suiting up for skiing with our pulks in tow. The towing harness goes on underneath our outer parkas to minimize time spent changing layers as the weather warms during the day (if it does).

Once we finish suiting up, we make a last check that all the gear is organized and ready to pack in the pulks. We drag the pulks into the vestibules and pack as efficiently as we can (Aaron is always faster than me at this). Finally, we step out of the tent to experience the weather outside for the first time of the day.

By the time we take down the tent and clear camp, we begin skiing at about 0600. It doesn't seem like the morning chores should take three hours, but we can rarely do much better in the bitter cold. To protect our hands from freezing, we wear liner gloves all the time. The only exception I can think of is when using toilet paper. In addition to liner gloves, we have to protect our hands with another heavier glove layer when handling sleep pads and stuff sacks. The cold nylon will quickly freeze hands through liner gloves even in the relative warmth of the tent, usually from 0°F to -10°F many mornings.

Aaron leads off the first shift of skiing this morning in conditions that are very tough to navigate. With the overcast and snowfall, the light is very flat. The lack of contrast makes finding something to ski toward difficult to impossible. We try to ski towards something on our compass bearing in travel a straight line. We want to travel in the most efficient way possible for us to get to the finish line. The new wind pattern continues. It is at our backs out of the southeast, making for more comfortable skiing than a headwind would.

Most of the first ski shift was a grinding climb through unconsolidated snow. Aaron seemed tired, yet he continued to lead the second shift. He is so much better at keeping us moving efficiently when the navigation conditions are tough. I took over the lead in the second half of the shift when the light improved so that Aaron could recover some.

It takes a surprising amount of extra energy to lead. There is the physical energy required to break the trail through the new snow. Then, there is the draining effect of using the mental energy required to keep maintain a compass bearing. This is all while done while we can't see the landscape in poor light over uneven ground. This all quickly saps our energy.

By the third ski shift, the light was much better. I take over the lead. The light wind blew ice crystals across our field of vision, creating sparkling "diamonds in the sky." With the changing light and gently blowing snow all day, we enjoyed some beautiful scenery.

By the fourth shift, snow started falling harder and blowing. Navigation again became difficult, so Aaron led. During the fifth and sixth ski shifts, we split up to ease the burden on Aaron. We again skied a "bonus" shift of 30 minutes at the end of the day. This was our strategy to make up for lost time and mileage. The downside of this approach is both Aaron and I are knackered at the end. I can't expect him to carry the extra weight of leading whenever navigation is hard. We are trying to keep our team of two moving as efficiently as we can.

Our slow progress the first week ate up all the storm days we built into our schedule. However, we haven't had any storm delays yet. How can we expect to spend a month on this ice cap without a storm delay? Yet at this rate, we'll have to keep moving regardless of weather in order to finish. I don't see how the daily mileage we're making will add up to us being able to finish before we are out of time and food.

Terry skiing in the morning across hard blue ice toward Camp 1
on the first full day of the expedition across Greenland.
(65° 51.29022'N, 39° 15.72648'W)

Who is Terry Williams?

My interest in adventure blossomed during my early high school years. I was born in central Ohio, the second son in a family headed by my father, a practically trained civil engineer for the town we lived in. He decided to re-enlist in the Navy when I was in middle school, and the Navy sent him to college to earn a degree in engineering. I remember the tough classes almost defeating my dad, but he made it to graduation.

My dad's first real assignment filled me with excitement. Until now, I had only lived in central Ohio and we had a two-year stint in North Chicago. But now, we were moving to Subic Bay in the Philippine Islands. I remember how strange everything felt. Even the humid tropical air seemed foreign.

When I walked downstairs to go to bed for the first time, exhausted from the long flights, there was a large gecko lizard perched on my pillow. I'm not sure if I'd ever seen a lizard before— just frogs and salamanders in our neighborhood creek in Ohio, but not lizards in the house!

But, I remember adjusting fairly quickly. I told my dad early on that since we were living in such a beautiful tropical place. I wanted to learn to SCUBA dive. He looked into it and could get me into a class with a group of Navy recruits, several of whom wanted eventually to train in the SEAL program. I loved the challenge of the class and I realized later that the men in the class were all looking out for me like I was their little brother back home.

Once I was certified, I found a friend at school who was older and had a driver's license and a car. We would routinely load our dive gear in his trunk in the morning, go to school, and then after school, we would drive to the end of the runway to dive at the reefs there. We drained our tanks looking for shells and lobster. Then, we refilled our tanks on the way home (no charge on base) and went home for a shower, dinner, and homework. It was paradise for a freshman in high school!

I feel fortunate that I was just young enough to not be interested in girls very much yet, but mature enough to enjoy the outdoors. I spent many hours diving or snorkeling in the warm, clear waters of the Philippines, and have a great fondness for the place and its people to this day.

After Dad's two-year tour in the Philippines, he received orders for Vietnam for one year, so the Navy moved my mom and siblings to a small house in Camarillo, California, for my junior year of high school. When he came home from Vietnam, his next orders were for a two-year tour at the Naval Air Station in Bermuda, so I was off to another paradise! Unfortunately, I learned that school there would be a challenge.

I would be in a senior class of four students and would have to take all of my AP classwork by correspondence. So, I had a tough conversation with my parents about leaving home a year early and arranged to live with the widowed grandmother of a high school girlfriend on a citrus farm back in Camarillo.

I will be forever grateful to this wonderful lady who was so courageous about taking in a teenage boy she'd never met and was so generous and loving to me. I worked as a busboy at a local restaurant to pay the modest board she charged, bought a Honda 350 motorcycle to get around on and I had a great senior year.

Next came undergraduate studies at UC San Diego. I chose this university because of its proximity to the Scripps Institute of Oceanography. Of course, after my experiences living and diving in the Philippines and Bermuda, I wanted to be an oceanographer. During my freshman year, I realized I would be more happy doing something in science where I could also have more human interactions.

I considered going into medicine. I didn't think I had what it took to make the grade, but another premed student challenged me to test myself by taking a heavy academic load and see if I could ace the classes, and I did, so I became a premed student.

The next few years brought lots of change and maturation to my life. I found my faith in Christ during a summer in Bermuda when a fellow lifeguard invited me to church with him. When I returned to UCSD in the fall, I met my future wife, Diane at a church college group Bible Study. We married the summer before my senior year and lived as paupers in married student housing, somehow getting by on her salary and my part-time work in an organic chemistry lab.

Medical school application time was stressful and expensive, draining any funds we had in the bank, but in the end, I was accepted to the UCSD School of Medicine. Because we didn't have to relocate for medical school, I was able to splurge and spend money on our first color TV with a 12-inch screen!

I enjoyed so many fields of study in medicine, that choosing a specialty was difficult. I ended up realizing that the part of patient care that I enjoyed most was that initial encounter when you had to put together often incomplete information, come up with a working diagnosis or a list of possible diagnoses (we call this a differential diagnosis), and begin treatment based on the most likely disease process.

What I learned I didn't enjoy was the daily hospital rounds where medications were tweaked and adjusted, and patients' conditions changed slowly. I also found that I enjoyed and was gifted with procedures. Given these preferences, I was drawn to the relatively new specialty of Emergency Medicine. Several department heads called me into their offices to tell me that my intellect and skills would be wasted in Emergency Medicine, but I wasn't dissuaded and ended up being accepted into one of the best Emergency Medicine residencies in the country at the time, UCSF Fresno.

By now, our family had grown to four with the birth of our first two daughters. We didn't enjoy living in Fresno very much, but when I had a rare day or two off, we'd drive to Yosemite Valley and enjoy the outdoors there together.

When my residency ended three years later, I took a job with the Kaiser system in Sacramento where I spent my entire career working in busy urban ERs full time. Our family grew to six with the addition of another girl and finally, we added our boy by adoption.

As a family, we were able to do some medical missionary work together with the desperately poor Guatemalans. The people I treated lived in and around the Guatemala City dump. We did other missions work in Northern India and Thailand. I also could fit in part-time work on cruise ships as a working vacation in the last half of my career, so despite the demands of my career, I continued to have adventures through this mission work and worldwide travel.

While working in Northern California, I took up whitewater kayaking on our backyard rivers, and those trips expanded to running rivers all over California and in Oregon. Eventually, I even kayaked the Colorado River through the Grand Canyon. My kayaking buddies also became partners in other adventures—alpine climbs in the Cascades, Bolivia, and Chile, backpacks and rock climbs in the Sierra, off-trail Sierra crossings, mountain biking adventures and misadventures, and more.

I had to wait until retirement to do something I'd dreamed about for years. I wanted to join a good friend and medical school classmate at a missionary hospital in the central highlands of Papua New Guinea. Finally, I could do that for three months on two separate trips in 2017. It was some of the most challenging and rewarding medicine that I've been involved in, and a wonderfully important spiritual time for me, as I had to learn to be more dependent on God for strength when my strength and skills were inadequate.

All of this is to explain where the roots of my love for the outdoors and outdoor adventure came from. Aaron's story and background are very different.

Terry on the summit of Aconcagua, Argentina. (22,841 ft / 6,960 m).
February 2005

Who is Aaron Linsdau?

"Your grandfather and his brother could walk across three wilderness ridges in an afternoon without a compass or map," my father shared with me one night.

"How did they find their way back?" I asked.

My dad smiled with the twinkle of a long-lost memory in his mind. "They just knew."

My family was full of outdoorsmen and women. Hunting, fishing, and camping were as normal to them as breathing. They were nomadic, finding work in the woods as lumberjacks and stone masons.

I experienced none of that.

When I was young, my parents lived in northwest Wyoming. They enjoyed as much of the adventure of skiing, hunting, and roaming the woods as they could. But, it was a tough life just getting by.

For as much enjoyment as my family had in the wilds of Wyoming, one brutal late-1970s winter of -60° Fahrenheit ended their desire for snow. Soon, my parents moved their young family to sunny San Diego. They traded six long months of winter for flip-flops and palm trees.

As I was young, I knew little of the outdoors my parents grew up with. Instead, I enjoyed the perfect weather Southern California upbringing. It was easy to be physically active in the outdoors in school but for one problem. I had asthma. Sometimes it was severe enough that I was completely unable to breathe.

My parents spent a day every few months taking me to doctors for my asthma while I was in elementary school. The hope was to see if there was a cure or at least a better method of relief than just an inhaler. After a few years of this approach, we found one doctor who seemed promising.

We had several visits with this doctor. It didn't take too long before he told my mother the bad news. "There is simply nothing to do. Your son won't be able to play sports and be active like other children."

There it was. The curse of not being normal. My mom says she doesn't remember that conversation. I remember it to this day.

I vowed I would change the course of my life.

In middle school, I made friends and took up volleyball. My being unable to breathe was a secret I kept hidden by excuses and maneuvering while playing as hard as I could. As I was in the Boy Scouts of America program, I had another outlet to work on myself in the outdoors.

All throughout junior high and high school, I struggled. But, bit by bit, I became better. Sometimes I would have an attack and have to use an inhaler, but I kept that under wraps. By the time I was studying electrical engineering in college, I rarely had an asthma attack.

Now, I was confident I could expand my horizons.

During one winter, an unusual amount of snow fell in the San Diego mountains. Listening to my parents' Wyoming winter stories for years inspired my brother and me. We went winter camping in the Laguna mountains. How tough could it be?

We froze.

Shivering in our inadequate San Diego clothing, we sat in the car a midnight running the heater. It never got warm. That was the end of my brother's winter camping excursions. However, I found unexpected joy in the challenge's suffering.

It took years before I camped again. It was always in the back of my mind. Early in my engineering career, I needed an escape from the stress. The thought of my Boy Scout backpacking days came to my mind. One place beckoned me—the Sierras.

My first solo forays into that iconic mountain range were a struggle. I learned to pack less, go lighter, and walk farther. After a few years, I found out how far I could go. Driving six hours from San Diego to Kings Canyon in Friday traffic, I escaped.

I spent the next two days backpacking forty miles. Then, I drove home, often returning at 3 a.m. Monday morning. After sleeping a few hours, I was back at work at 7 a.m.

Asthma was a distant bad dream.

Once I had the fast packing down, I expanded to winter camping in the Sierras. One unexpectedly cold night was 5ºF (-15ºC). I shivered in my sleeping bag. This was all before YouTube, so I had to ask around until I found proper cold-weather expedition equipment.

This led me to my first foray into solo Arctic trekking in Greenland in October 2008. A single-page Backpacker Magazine article on inspired me. I traveled for three days to Kangerlussuaq, Greenland via Copenhagen, Denmark. I bought camp fuel and maps at an airport supply store and hired a driver for $120 USD to take me to the trail head. There, I set off on a 100-mile (160 km) solo trek across the Arctic tundra. It was a risky late-season trek. Greenland authorities warned me an Arctic blizzard could trap me. It snowed for a few days, so I was lucky. It only dropped to -25ºF (-32ºC), right at the edge of my gear's capability.

I fell in love with the experience and was hooked.

A year later, I happened to watch a National Geographic special on Yellowstone National Park in the winter. Photographer Tom Murphy hiked through the deep winter to create his iconic photographs. I called him. To my amazement, he spent an hour with me, imparting wisdom.

For the next three years, I trekked hundreds of miles across Yellowstone in the winter. Temperatures dropped to -45ºF (-43ºC) on each expedition. I was ready for something bigger.

All the while, stress at my engineering job had reached an all-time high. America was still recovering from the 2008 global financial crisis. It was non-stop pressure. I developed chest and jaw pain.

During one fateful Friday dentist appointment in spring, the dentist said I shattered two fillings from grinding my teeth from stress. That expensive multi-hour visit changed the course of my life.

Dying from a stroke or heart attack wasn't worth it for the nice paycheck. The following Monday, I put in my notice. Over a few weeks, I sold and stored much of what I had. Soon, I moved to Jackson Hole, Wyoming to train for an expedition I had always dreamt of.

By the fall of 2012, I set out for Antarctica. I hoped to ski alone to the South Pole and back from the edge of the continent.

It didn't go as planned.

I coughed up blood. A lung infection nearly wiped me out. My sleds and shovel broke from the extreme cold. After 81 days alone, it was the best time of my life. I had also set a world record for surviving the longest solo expedition to the South Pole.

Once I returned home, I had a major problem. What would I do now?

The corporate world wasn't for me anymore. It was like starting life all over again. I cast about for inspiration. Several people told me I should write a book about my experience, as I was lucky to have made it at all. I'd never written a book and no one else I knew had. It took me a year to write *Antarctic Tears*.

That book enabled me to build a career as a motivational speaker, author, professional explorer, and filmmaker. This life was dramatically different from engineering and yet it was similar. I am still creating, just in another form.

On one fateful trip to climb Kilimanjaro in 2016, my flight from

San Francisco to Amsterdam canceled. The gate agent informed me another person was in the same predicament. He was also traveling to Tanzania to climb Kilimanjaro. That's when I met the affable Dr. Terry Williams, M.D. After a brief conversation, we discovered we were on the same expedition. Soon, we became fast friends.

After that expedition, I solo climbed Denali in Alaska twice, climbed Mt. Elbrus in Russia, and trekked the States, climbing and hiking to many high points. Meanwhile, I started my YouTube channel and released a series of adventure guidebooks. My new life expanded more and more after retiring from engineering.

The pandemic put a pause on my international travel. But, I continued to do what I could in the US. The adventure bug was a permanent infection. I shared my outdoor knowledge with others via video and books.

Terry and I stayed in contact over the years. We went on two Yellowstone winter training expeditions. We were preparing for my next big dream—crossing the Greenland ice cap.

Aaron at the South Pole, Antarctica. (9,301 ft / 2,835 m).
January 2013

An Unlikely Meeting

How do a 49-year-old polar explorer and professional adventurer and a 68-year-old retired Emergency Medicine doctor meet and become intergenerational friends? Here's our story.

In the summer of 2015, I heard about a trip to Tanzania to climb Mt. Kilimanjaro that some of my Northern California friends were going on, and I decided to join them. At one of the flight layovers, I was called up to the counter to be told that the next leg of the flight was canceled, and the Airline representative introduced me to another traveler who was also headed for Tanzania. That's the short story of how I met Aaron, a polar explorer and only the second American to ski solo from the coast of Antarctica to the South Pole. We immediately figured out that we were on the same expedition, to climb Mt. Kilimanjaro on a guided trip.

We decided to keep traveling as far as Amsterdam that day. The idea was that in case of other delays, we would at least be in Europe and within striking distance of Tanzania. I had traveled there before while doing cruise ship medicine, so it was a chance to take my new friend into the old city and give him a walking tour. We enjoyed the time together and returned to our hotel to get some needed sleep after the jet lag of crossing the Atlantic.

Fortunately, the next day, we were able to travel on to Tanzania and join our group in time for the start of the climb. The rest of the group had already organized into tent mates, so Aaron and I, being the last to arrive became tent mates. Both of us had backpacked enough to be aware of what it takes to share a cramped tent space without getting on each other's nerves. It turns out that awareness started us out on the right foot for spending a lot more time out in the wilderness together in the future.

The pace of life on the climb was very pleasant and left room for acclimatization, rest, and conversation. Our guides came around in the morning to see that we were awake in time and passed in a tray of tea and coffee (very civilized!). Then, we would dress in our hiking clothes and head to the mess tent for breakfast.

Meanwhile, the guides would move in behind us and take down our tents and pack up our heavier gear bags, while we each were left with a light day pack to carry for the day. The guides would move ahead of us carrying those heavy loads and the next camp would be set up for us by the time we arrived at the end of the trail for the day.

Each evening and morning, Aaron and I had plenty of time to chat and get to know each other. I learned of his background: he was trained as an engineer but retired from that career to make a living as a professional adventurer, motivational speaker, YouTube channel publisher and author. I peppered him with questions about his Antarctic epic in 2013, when he dragged two pulks loaded with gear for over 720 miles over 81 days from the coast of Antarctica to the South Pole.

His original plan was to do the round trip to the pole and back to the coast, but he was foiled by terrible conditions and a bout of pneumonia that slowed his progress to a crawl on many days. I promised myself that I'd get a copy of his book, *Antarctic Tears*, and read about his epic myself.

During one of our conversations in the tent, Aaron told me about his plans to write a book about how to plan your own expedition. He let me know that a missing piece was someone with the expertise to write the medical section of the book. Now that I was retired, I felt I had the time to take on a project like that. I didn't have any expectations about making money off the project, but hoped that by getting that kind of exposure, possibly other large and well funded-expeditions would consider me as a candidate to be their expedition doctor. After our successful climb of Kilimanjaro, we worked hard on the project and published *Adventure Expedition One* together in 2019.

Aaron (left) and Terry at Camp 0, Greenland Ice Cap. (3,000 ft / 914 m).
April 23, 2023

The Greenland Crossing Expedition

Aaron and I continued our friendship. We stayed in contact even though I live in North San Diego County and he has lived in Jackson, WY, the Oregon coast, and Idaho in the last several years. He travels to San Diego regularly to visit his parents who live south of the city.

On one of these visits, Diane and I met Aaron and his girlfriend Kelly at a local sports bar that has great beer and food. Aaron mentioned during lunch that his adventure wish list includes a ski crossing of the Greenland ice cap at the Arctic Circle. He has done a solo trip to Greenland before to hike the Arctic Circle trail out of Kangerlussuaq on the west coast.

Aaron loves to do solo expeditions where he has no one to rely on but himself. Besides his Antarctic epic, he has skied solo many times through Yellowstone National Park in the winter and has done many solo hikes and climbs in the west. But there was a barrier to his dream of doing the ice cap. Greenland authorities do not allow solo expeditions across the ice cap.

I'm a fairly experienced cross-country and backcountry skier and snow camper. I've done lots of winter camping and alpine climbs through the years. Diane and I learned to cross-country ski together when our family was young. We went as often as we could, even taking the young kids in tow. Diane even skied with me out the Glacier Point road in Yosemite to camp at Glacier Point. We wanted to wake up to the sunrise across the canyon to Half Dome! The best part—Diane did this when she was 7 months pregnant!

I have had a longtime fascination with polar exploration and have read extensively about the Golden Age of Polar Exploration. The idea or even a desire to test myself in the high latitudes never crossed my mind. When Aaron mentioned his idea of a Greenland ice cap crossing expedition at lunch that day, I looked at Diane for approval.

At that moment, I wasn't sure Aaron knew if he intended that to be an invitation to join him on a Greenland expedition. If it was, I was all in. Diane gave me a look that said, "OK, go for it if that's what you want."

So, that's how it began. We started planning together. My first task was to outfit myself with gear to survive the conditions we expected. Using Aaron's Antarctic experience and advice, we built a list of needed gear. I started watching for sales. We also knew that it was important to train for the Arctic conditions together. Testing gear was important so that we didn't take any untested gear onto the ice cap.

We met in Wyoming in January 2020, to ski into Yellowstone together for a week on our first training expedition. Our goal was to test ourselves. The weather cooperated!

The rangers actually closed the park entrance behind us. They expected an Arctic storm, but they knew Aaron and his polar experience, so they let us continue with our planned ski trip. Each of us pulled a heavy pulk. I was liberal with packing extra gear to test, knowing that in Greenland the pulks would be much heavier.

We had brilliant weather for our purpose. Yellowstone delivered low temperatures, less than -20°F, high winds, and blowing snow. The main gear failure I experienced was the fur ruff that I had hand-sewn on my hood disintegrated. When I returned home, the company that sold me the ruff was kind enough to help me upgrade from fox to wolverine. They gave me a discount on having one of their professionals sew it on for me. On our next training trip in March 2021, all the gear performed well.

The COVID pandemic delayed our timetable for the expedition. We knew that the travel to Greenland would be expensive and challenging enough. The different and fluctuating vaccination, isolation, and quarantine requirements made us delay our plans.

Traveling through multiple countries to reach Greenland would cost us weeks of quarantine time. We delayed our plans until 2023. We learned that by April 2023, the COVID-related restrictions eased so we could travel freely.

We both had been physically training for months, staying in good overall shape with hikes, runs, and bike rides, as well as strength work. As the expedition approached, we added tire-dragging sessions a few times a week in order to simulate the pulk dragging that we would be doing. Dragging tires is a tedious workout. It's not a very fun workout. But, we faced long days of pulling pulks through the snow day after day for a month. Unfortunately, there is no way to truly simulate skiing over 9 hours a day with training in a city. We did our best.

Being older and smaller than Aaron, he must have had concerns about how I would do with the heavier pulk. Adventuring together involves trust and mutual respect. I appreciate Aaron trusted me to show up in shape to complete the task we faced.

The permitting process for an ice cap crossing is complex and long. Even though we followed Greenland's recommended permit timetable, we didn't begin it soon enough. Everything took far longer than expected.

One part of the permit that the Greenland authorities required is search and rescue insurance. We went through three companies before we found one that met their requirements. Each aborted attempt cost us more than a week in time. We were also required to provide resumés of our experience and a medical clearance for me, the elder team member.

We had to provide bank guarantees for payment. This was required in case of an evacuation not due to an emergency or a search and rescue. It took a week to arrange this with the bank.

We not only needed multiple emergency communication devices, but we also had to submit radio permits to use them. The communications gear included two expensive satellite phones, a marine radio, and a personal locator beacon. The prepaid phone SIM cards cost $3 USD per minute. We needed two of these with 75 minutes preloaded each. This added up to nearly $500 alone.

We needed to carry crevasse rescue equipment, too. Each of us assembled a kit that enabled us to ascend a rope if uninjured. The other part of the kit was to haul our injured partner out of a crevasse with a z-pully setup.

We each carried a GPS device and a global compass for navigation. The GPS units worked well in the Arctic. Navigating during the day with compasses in the extreme cold added to the challenge.

One piece of gear that we couldn't have fail was our stove. Every day, we had to melt snow to make our daily drinking water. Failure would bring a quick end to our expedition. We decided to each bring a stove. They were identical MSR XGK expedition models. We had a backup fuel bottle, a spare pump, and a full repair kit.

On the first night, we were glad that we each brought a stove. We ended up running both stoves in the evenings. This saved time and got us to sleep earlier. The stoves performed flawlessly for over a month.

Once our permit finally came through a mere three weeks before our expedition window, we bought our airline tickets. We routed to Greenland through Reykjavik, Iceland. Both of us scrambled to arrange lodging and logistics on each end of the crossing.

By late April, we had our gear packed. Aaron and I flew to Salt Lake City where we met up to regroup and travel on the next day. Our flights took us through New York and on to Keflavik, Iceland. We rapidly transitioned from the luxury of hotel beds and daily showers to the stark reality that our life on the ice cap would become.

The next day, we flew from Keflavik, Iceland, to a tiny frozen gravel airstrip at Kulusuk on Greenland's east coast. We finally were on the ground. But, fog grounded our scheduled helicopter flight from Kulusuk to Tasilaq overnight.

The delay forced us to scramble to reschedule our flight from Tasilaq up onto the ice cap. We lost a day an entire day. We had to manage the final logistics of buying fuel, packing our pulks, and renting a shotgun, in a short 8-hour window.

It turns out that the delay led to some pleasant new friendships. Kulusuk is such a small village that there aren't many rooms in the only hotel. Air Greenland housed us in an old lodge building that many of the airport workers live in. The woman who helped us get settled was the sister of the airport gate agent who we worked with. Christine was a delight to get to know.

Over coffee in the morning, she taught us about polar bear behavior. Christine told us that for the first time in her life, she had seen narwhal in their bay when the ice cleared last summer. Aaron and I will forever be grateful for the delay that gave us the chance to meet these hardy siblings.

The next day, we rode to the airstrip in a pickup full of airport workers. One of them was armed with a rifle in case of polar bear encounters. We waited until late afternoon for the spectacular short flight to a nearby island where the Tasilaq heliport is located. I had arranged to stay at The Red House since they have a reputation for assisting ice cap crossing expeditions.

It turns out that the lodge's owner, Robert, has crossed the ice cap thirteen times! One crossing was a round trip. Another was a crossing at the widest point in Greenland, hundreds of miles north of our route. He accomplished his fastest crossing in 12 days with the help of dog teams.

We asked him to sit down with us and advise us on mistakes he had seen teams make so that we could avoid them. Later, when I sat down with Robert to settle our bill, he wished us the best. He said that we would need some luck. But, he encouraged me that crossing the ice cap is a fantastic experience with no equal. We will be a solitary speck in the middle of a vast wilderness.

During our rushed preparation day, we hiked down to the fuel depot near the harbor. We bought heptane stove fuel in a 20-liter jug. It was grueling to haul the 40 pounds of fuel back to the Red House. We tested the fuel in our stoves to make sure it was good. Then, we transferred the 13 liters we needed for a month to our fuel containers and packed the bottles in our pulks.

Aaron and I also had to visit the local police station. We had to give them information about our expedition. We provided satellite phone numbers, emergency contacts, our planned route, and how many days of supplies we had.

Robert rented us a shotgun and ammunition for polar bear defense. He gave us tips on dealing with bears. His disconcerting advice was to allow the bear to get uncomfortably close, about 50 feet (15 meters), before firing a warning shot in the air. If the bear was farther away, it would not retreat.

The key piece of information was how the bear would act. If it stopped moving around with its nose in the air, we had a problem. This sniffing behavior indicates they are smelling and trying to figure out what we are. If it then crouched down low with its eyes focused on us, we needed to load the shotgun with a lethal slug round. We had to be prepared to shoot to kill. This change in behavior means that the bear intends to charge and kill us!

Once we had our expedition gear packed, our last chore was to bundle up our travel clothes, shoes, ski bags, and gear duffels and haul them down to the heliport. We had to ship them by air freight to Old Camp at Kangerlussuaq on the west coast where we planned to stay. With our chores complete, we returned to the Red House for a last shower and some food. We had a few hours to wait before our 6:15 p.m. charter flight to our starting point on the ice cap.

The Red House staff helped us transport our heavy pulks in a trailer to the heliport. Loaded with all of our food, fuel, tent, shotgun, and water for the first time, they were intimidatingly heavy. At the heliport, Aaron's pulk with the tent weighed in at 69 kilos (150.6 pounds). Mine with the shotgun and ammo weighed in at 73 kilos (160 pounds).

Robert had suggested our pulks should weigh no more than 60 kilos (132 pounds).

We chose a starting point at about 3,000 feet elevation on the ice cap. That starting point was north of the tiny village of Isortoq. We wanted to bypass the rough terrain at the edge of the ice cap. The short flight was spectacular. When the pilot set the helicopter down, he rammed it onto the ice surface while at full power in order to check for hidden crevasses.

The pilot and copilot helped us unload our heavy pulks. We took a few pictures with big smiles. The crew lifted off. Rotor wash blew Aaron's ski poles past us.

As the helicopter flew away, the reality of the situation set in. We were in the silence of the ice cap for the first time. We pitched our tent at Camp 0 at 2,999-foot elevation. Soon, we cooked dinner. This was our first of many nights on the ice.

I was nervous about the monumental task we faced. Tomorrow our compass bearing is 286° to our first landmark. We planned to ski toward the Cold War-era abandoned missile tracking station, DYE-2, 286 miles away.

The Journals

Both Aaron and I kept expedition journals to document the trip. Being one of the oldest teams to cross the ice cap, we believed the record would be useful to future explorers. Soon, those journals became more than that.

What we discovered during the journey across Greenland was that their different perspectives would offer insight into their experience. This pair of late-middle-aged polar explorers had to overcome countless obstacles. The toughest weren't the deep snow, bitter cold, or freezing winds. Instead, they had to manage the most difficult of challenges for humans—maintaining a positive relationship.

We encountered fresh polar bear tracks early on. This scared us into the reality of the experience. Knowing there was a minor but possible chance of facing death by an animal made the experience real. This was new to me. The added stress of the danger made the already difficult experience that much more rewarding.

Contained beyond here is a collection of my and Aaron's journals in facing-page format. The reader will be able to see both of our perspectives side-by-side. Me, being a doctor and Aaron, being an engineer, gave us different perspectives.

Many days are the same in the Arctic. Other days are wild and never to be repeated. This is like the life humans experience. We hope you learn about what it takes to maintain a friendship in the toughest environment on Earth.

My journal entries are on the left pages. Aaron's entries are on the right pages in a different font. The reader can compare our perspectives during the expedition. The text of the journals is lightly edited to provide the reader with the polar travel experience.

Sunday, April 16, 2023 (Terry)

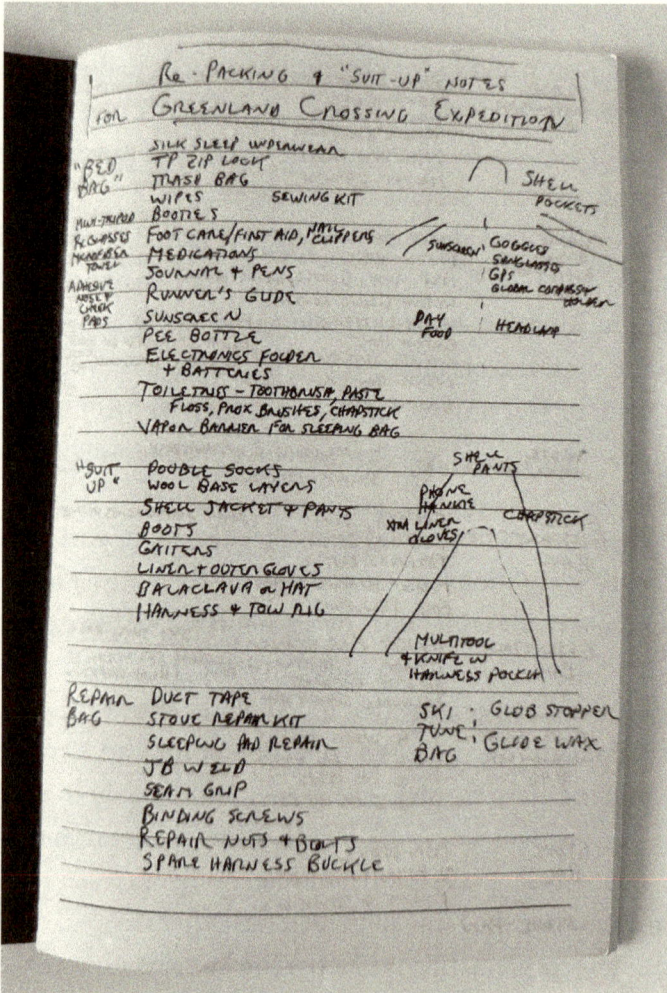

Terry's journal with his packing plan.

Sunday, April 16, 2023 (Aaron)

Flew from northern Idaho at noon to Salt Lake City with a big duffel, sled, bag, and ski bag all loaded to fifty pounds each. All heavy but good. I upgraded to First Class with SkyMiles on Delta to take care of any possible problems. (First Class passengers seem to get a different treatment). I watched Kelly stand at the fence as she saw me off at the plane ramp. She's such a good woman.

I'm still feeling the fatigue of a cold that hit me on April 11. On April 12, I went crazy taking Vitamin C to try and crush it. I probably caught the cold at Easter brunch on April 9 (2023) at the restaurant at near home. We were blessed it stayed at a low-level cold.

I was worried it would turn into bronchitis and then pneumonia. I stayed up too late Monday morning (April 3) doing paperwork at the last minute. Classic mistake.

The flight from home to Salt Lake City was uneventful.

I got to Salt Lake City, caught a shuttle to Salt Lake City Airport Springhill Suites, and met with my expedition partner, Terry Williams, at the hotel. He had arrived earlier and gotten to the room. We ordered Uber Eats from Black Bear Diner and enjoyed our last dinner in America. We didn't want to expose ourselves to other people to reduce the chance of illness.

Aaron waving goodbye as he departs from home for nearly two months.

Linsdau/Williams Greenland Crossing (Terry)

17 April, 2023
JFK Airport, NYC

Travel started yesterday with a morning flight from San Diego to Salt Lake City where I met Aaron at an airport hotel to regroup and then travel on.

But, preparation began years ago… The idea for this joint expedition was hatched at lunch together at LTH (Local Tap House) in Oceanside about 3 years ago. Aaron mentioned his desire to do this trip, but his "thing" is solo trips, but Greenland doesn't allow solo crossings of the ice cap. I've always been interested in polar exploration, so I volunteered my partnership.

We did training skis together in Yellowstone, skiing from the South Entrance. The first was in Arctic storm conditions, with wind, blowing snow, and subzero temperatures—so a good test, for me particularly. I've learned a lot from Aaron about travel and camping in harsh winter conditions, and this built on that experience.

Today we flew from SLC to JFK, and had a long layover before flying on to Reykjavik overnight tonight. Have had to take care of some last-minute logistics: Confirming that we indeed paid for our radio permit in Greenland, Pre-paying for our overweight bags with Greenland Air (to save 30%), etc.

We go on to Iceland tonight, we begin our transition from the luxury of hotel beds, showers, and airport lounges to the stark reality of the Greenland ice cap.

Monday, April 17, 2023 (Aaron)

Breakfast at the Marriott Springhill was good. It's always a great choice to fire us up. Schlepping our huge bags, we took the shuttle to the airport and made our way to the Delta lounge at the Salt Lake airport. The lounge access pays off super well with endless food and drinks, plus comfort. Enjoying a last mimosa was a special treat.

We enjoyed a 4.5 hour flight from Salt Lake City (SLC) to JFK airport in New York in coach with middle seats. That was not fun. There were just no upgrades or better seats available when we booked our flights a few weeks ago. The flight was nearly fully loaded when I booked it.

There was also one woman who delayed the plane demanding her roll-aboard be placed in the overhead. There was simply no room. She had clearly booked a basic economy ticket or lower-rate ticket. She boarded last but clearly wasn't happy with the result.

The flight was uneventful. Arriving at JFK, we made our way to the Delta lounge in Terminal 4. It didn't take long to make it to the lounge where we stayed until 10 p.m. when our flight boarded.

We caught our flight to Iceland! The 757 was comfortable with the upgrade to Comfort Plus. That made a big difference with the food and drinks provided. Terry didn't have trouble with legroom in coach but for me, a few inches on the knees is a big deal. I knew once we hit the ground, we'd be working hard.

I got dehydrated on the plane. Oops. I was trying to balance choking out from lack of water and having to hit the lavatory a dozen times on the flight. The second option would have been a better choice.

The red-eye flight from JFK to Reykjavik felt longer than I'd expected. I did get some sleep, though it wasn't great. I had too much anticipation running through my head.

Tuesday, 18 April 18, 2023 (Terry)
B&B Guesthouse, Keflavik

Travel continues to go smoothly. After hanging around the Delta lounge at JFK, eating and drinking all we could hold, we boarded and flew 5 hours through the very short night to KEF airport in Iceland.

We arrived too early for the guest house to pick us up, so we took a public bus for $3.67 (500 ISK) for the 2 of us. The bus driver forgot us and drove past our bus stop, so had to schlep 150 pounds each down the street in stages. But, they were nice enough to put us in our room early, so we napped.

Aaron needed more sleep so I snuck out and walked along the waterfront for an hour. Very pretty, but overcast, windy, and cool. And some sprinkles. Neat, tidy, modest houses in this fishing town. Sea walls built of lava rocks that flowed 200k years ago. Most plentiful seabirds were the Eider ducks. They're white & black, plump diving birds that eat mussels.

Aaron (left) and Terry at the Leif Erikson monument in the Keflavik Airport, the gateway to Reykjavik and Iceland.

Tuesday, April 18, 2023 (Aaron)

We arrived at KEF (Keflavik), the Reykjavik airport! We aren't even going to get into the capital city because it's an hour from the airport. Terry booked a lodging for us not too far from the airport, saving time and money. Plus, it reduces stress.

The best part is all of our bags arrived. That was huge. It would've been cheaper to ship our equipment, but we only had eighteen days to put this all together. Our permit literally came through at the last moment. The $280 fee for the third checked bag was painful.

We went through the customs green line, meaning nothing to declare. We walked straight toward a one-way window. The immigration officer lady gave me a hard time about only staying one day in Iceland. Terry looked like he had no trouble or needed to explain. She grilled me on entry and exit dates. I look like a criminal while Terry is a perfect angel. It must be his youthful looks.

It took a bit to get our luggage since it was oversized. We found FREE luggage carts. That's the thing about other countries—luggage carts are free at the airport. In America, they charge $4–$6. Glad Terry had this figured out well beforehand.

We caught the #55 bus to Keflavik in a big tour bus. We had no trouble getting our gear into the bus's huge underbelly. Terry had figured all the bus arrangements out, saving us on a hefty taxi fee.

Our bus driver missed our stop right next to the guest house Terry had arranged. We had to haul our gear about 400 yards. That was super tough, triple-hauling three bags at 50 pounds each. It was a good expedition mental and physical training.

The couple who own the guest house are from Poland and they have a daughter going to school here. They're looking to sell and move back to warmer climates. They're both quite nice.

While Terry went for a walk to the waterfront, I took a nap. I feel like I'm battling the onset of a cold. A man behind me at the Easter buffet literally sneezed all over me, sending a germ cloud four days from departure.

Wednesday, April 19, 2023 (Terry)
Kulusuk Airport, East Greenland

All went smoothly this morning. Breakfast, then we took a van to the airport, checked bags, then about a 2-hour smooth flight in a small turboprop to this airport (KUS). There's low overcast with fog and a light drizzle, the temperature right above freezing.

The helicopter on to Tasilaq is delayed by weather, so as the Greenlandic flight attendant said, "We wait."

Meanwhile, our bags sit on the wet mud/gravel taxiway in the drizzle. Hopefully not enough to soak things through.

Met a retired rheumatologist from Kaiser/ROS who is here to ski tour with a group named Paul Lambie. I'll need to connect with him after I get home.

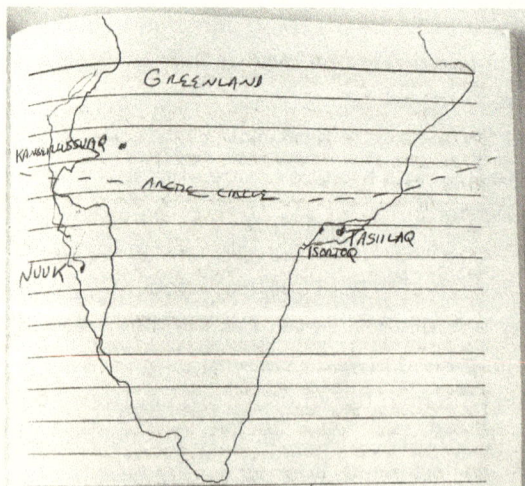

Terry's expedition route sketch.

We met Benj who is the airport worker who helped us when our flight to Tasilaq was canceled. When he heard we're planning to cross the ice cap, he became very animated and interested. He asked us to email him once we were finished.

Wednesday, April 19, 2023 (Aaron)

Terry and I were up and tired. The midnight sun made sleep difficult for me, though Terry seemed to have no trouble. He definitely travels better than I do. It must be all those years as a doctor. He could probably sleep through anything.

Our breakfast at the guest house was good. Classic cold-cut meats, bread, and spread. This is what I really look forward to when traveling to European-style countries. What a great time.

The guest house had an airport shuttle. Nice.

I had read others had trouble with freight being late. Checking gear was expensive but we had all our stuff with us.

Our flight to Kulusuk was over an hour on a small twin turboprop. It was fun flying right at the Arctic Circle. The seats were small for my legs but Terry had no troubles. He said he enjoyed this part of being short.

We landed on a dirt strip in Kulusuk. The little town's main purpose was the airport, fishing, and fighting off polar bears. To our dismay, our flight to Tasilaq was, then canceled. Stuck at the airport.

A heli-ski group with a guide was also at the airport. They had their rifle already in Iceland so the guide didn't have to import back and forth from the U.S. Much simpler on this side.

We had emailed Daniel, one of the Air Greenland agents about arranging a helicopter ride to the ice cap. We realized we would have a tough time getting from Tasilaq to Isortoq on a once-a-week scheduled chopper on Thursday. We would have then to hire sled dogs to take us to the base of the ice cap. And then we'd have to haul up 3,000 feet to the other guided expedition starting points.

We quickly realized that'd be a mistake and changed plans. I emailed Air Greenland to arrange a helicopter ride to 1,000 meters (3,400 feet) up the ice cap. Terry had to figure out a few good GPS points to give them for a flight quote.

The airport put us up in at the airport staff house. It was okay because we were closer to the dock, so we could wander around. Christine, the lady who shepherded us, made sure we had some ramen with meat for dinner.

Terry and I set ourselves up, then wandered around. The whole

His coworker, Christina, is running the lodge (in the process of being reconstructed and refurbished). She got us comfortably settled, and once we learned her name, I told her that my Gramma was named Christine. She asked me to call her Gramma. We need to tell our friend in the U.S. that I have family in Kulusuk, Greenland.

There is a beautiful frozen fjord here. Christina said we can walk, but not far, because polar bears come sometimes.

The airport luggage guy drove us over to the lodge. He said that there was a seal on the ice today, the first time for this season.

After getting settled and eating a snack, we went for a beautiful walk. The fjord here is beautiful in this light and mist. We walked over to where most of the dogs are housed. They all stayed quiet and we stayed back. All are pretty, white huskies, one with a black face. Christina told us that they stay quiet because one of the workers who lives downstairs feeds them regularly.

We asked Christina more about polar bears. She told us the men in this village used to kill ~50/year. And now, the authorities limit them to 15/year. She said that makes them mad, because polar bears are really good to eat unless they are starving and skinny. She said she wished she could give us a taste, but it takes a long time to cook (trichinosis). To help us understand, she explained that they eat seals and polar bears, but we eat cows and chickens.

As I look out the window, I don't see any other food options in this Arctic wilderness. I asked her if the bears would kill their dogs, and she said "No," Bears enter the village because they are hungry.

One will trap someone in their house, and they'll call another man to come shoot it. The other tip she gave me: If I see a lot of blackbirds gathering, it's because there is a bear there.

Weather seems to be changing with the sky breaking up, so we're hopeful for being able to move on to Tasilaq tomorrow.

bay was frozen over with icebergs. What a forlorn location. They used to shoot 50 polar bears a year and eat/process them. "Big man" then came and said they could only shoot 15 polar bears a year. This has caused no end of grief because bears are a real danger here.

There were neat pencil drawings on the wall in my room. We both enjoyed one of the last showers.

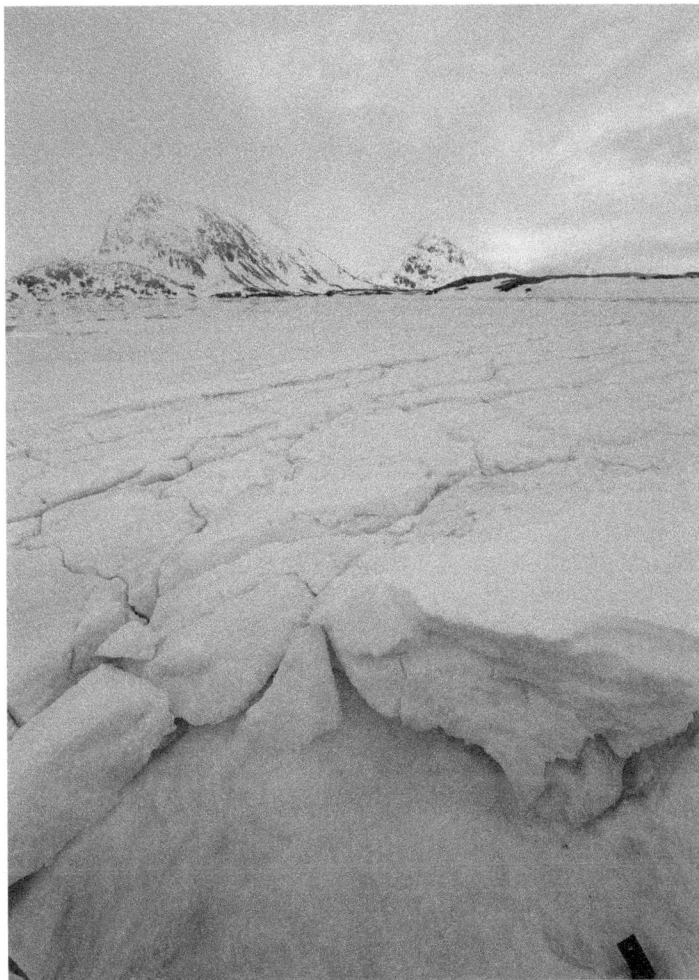

Frozen bay with iceberg at Kulusuk, Greenland.

Thursday, 20 April, 2023 (Terry)
Kulusk, Greenland

So quiet and peaceful here, having coffee with Christina and looking out at the still landscape and blue sky. No wildlife other than a few ravens. Dusk was at 21:30 last night and dawn began at 03:30. Should be flying today with it being so calm and clear.

Christina told us that Narwal appeared in the water to the north last year for the first time in her life. The village men took several of them for meat.

Terry excited to fly a Bell chopper from Kulusuk to Tasilaq, Greenland.

Thursday, April 20, 2023 (Aaron)

We were both up at 5 a.m, getting ready. We enjoyed the breakfast Christine cooked us. It was tasty and heartfelt. We were at the airport by 9 a.m. and ready to go. The helicopter picked us up and the others who stayed at the Kulusuk hotel.

We hadn't heard from Air Greenland about our ice cap flight drop-off. After I got my phone working on the Greenland cell network, we found our contact was out for several days. The guy on the line said we could just email and they'd figure it out eventually. We told him we needed to get this arranged now. He said he'd call back.

He called back pretty quickly with a quote. A mere $5,200 to get us to the ice cap. Ouch! A massive chunk of spending we'd not planned on. But after talking with people on the ground, we knew we needed to pay or it might take us 3–5 days to ascend the ice cap. And we were already pushing our time limit. So, Terry handed over his credit card. At least we had all the connections completed. Talk about taking it down to the last minute!

Pretty soon, the helicopter landed, we loaded up, and were in Tasilaq in 10 minutes. Our driver from The Red House picked us up. We met Robert the owner who'd done 13 crossings over the years. He's pretty famous for this. He told us to purchase Heptane at the fuel dump at the harbor. The camp store had no white gas!! It took us 5 hours to arrange our gear for flying tomorrow. It wasn't too stressful but we had to be careful.

Terry and I wandered and found the grocery store and made some boxed dinners in the expedition house at The Red House. It was nice to have it to ourselves being so early in the season. We finished prepping and went to sleep.

Friday, 21 April, 2023 (Terry)
The Red House
Tasilaq, Greenland

Spent the remainder of yesterday wiling away the time at the Kulusuk airport, waiting for our late afternoon flight. Beautiful clean weather. "Gramma" Christine took the best care of us she could, feeding us Danish hot dogs and snacks, sugary sodas, etc.

Turns out that Benj is her younger brother. 10 kids in their family!

The flight to Tasilaq was spectacular and too short. Ice capped islands surrounded by pancake ice, icebergs with the underwater portion glowing green—just beautiful.

Tasilaq is a much bigger town, with maybe 2,000 inhabitants. We checked into The Red House. They were nice enough to upgrade us to the "Expedition Hut" so we would have room to sort and pack—and that was a good thing.

We walked to the store to get DKK from the ATM, look for white gas (no luck), and bought frozen pizza and beer for dinner. Then spent the evening sorting, organizing, and packing pulks. Finally quiet at 22:30 and hit the sack—the last bed for 5 weeks!

After breakfast at The Red House & getting some tips from Robert (the owner and multiple-time Greenland crosser), we checked in at the police station (Robert called them and confirmed this was necessary). Then, we went to the larger store (still not white gas or heptane). We didn't panic because The Red House staff told us we could get it at the fuel depot.

The smallest quantity was 20L and we needed 13L each, so not too bad. It was about $130 USD.

Robert rented us a shotgun and gave us tips on dealing with polar bears:

Wait until they get close (15–20M) before firing a warning shot in the air.

If the bear stops moving and crouches low (like a pouncing cat), get ready to fire a lethal shot.

Friday, April 21, 2023 (Aaron)

We woke up early and made our way to the fuel depot. Another $250 later, we had 20 liters of heptane, a fuel that Robert said had more "oomph" than white gas. Carrying the 45-pound jug back to the lodge was an ordeal. We shared the load, swapping back and forth. This DIY style is definitely a lot of work.

We tested the fuel and our stoves fired up. It was a clean batch. Terry and I parceled our fuel into bottles and finished prepping our gear. We wrapped up the rest of our stuff and took it to the airport for freight. Again, another nearly $300 had our ski bags shipped to Kangerlussuaq to Old Camp Lodge. Hopefully it makes it!

I showed Terry how to use the satellite phone, VHF radio, and figure out what our schedule would be. After eating a box lunch, we were ready to go.

Unfortunately, the airport didn't have any food, so we went without dinner before launching. Hopefully that doesn't cost anything later.

Robert said to take the right side of the glacier. We should have asked him to show us on the map. We'd pay for that later.

Renting a shotgun with birdshot and slugs for polar bears was great. It solved the problem of another piece of luggage, permits, etc.

Aaron (left), Robert Peroni (middle), and Terry at The Red House in Tasilaq.

He also gave us tips on proper wall construction for a camp for a wind storm.

After schlepping the fuel jug to the cabin, Aaron tested the stove and we filled our bottles. We left the remaining 6–7L with them. We packed up our unneeded bags, clothes, and shoes (19kg) and shipped them to Kangerlussuaq by air freight (~$164), then finally went back to The Red House with chores done.

One last shower and now it's time to write while we wait for our 6:15 p.m. flight up on the ice cap.

I hope Aaron is finally relaxing now that all the logistics are done. I certainly have some last-minute butterflies—we're actually going on this adventure!

When I settled up our bill with Robert, he wished us the best & said that we would need some luck, but he reassured me that it is a fantastic experience with no equal. Being a solitary speck in the middle of a 360° vast wilderness.

Terry filling up with his last civilized meal before the expedition.

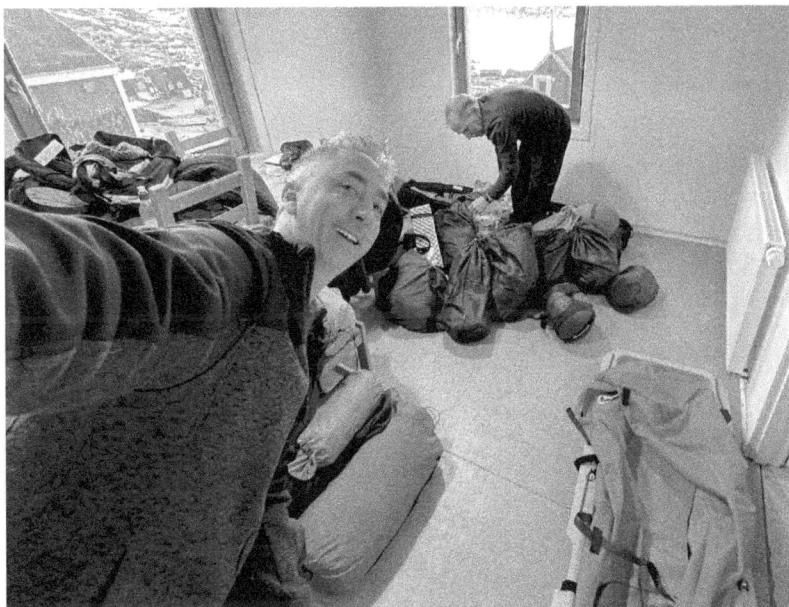

Aaron clicking a photo while Terry prepares his 152 pounds (68 kg) of gear.

Pilot (left), Terry (middle), and Aaron at their helicopter drop point.

21 April, 2023 (Terry)
21:40
Camp 0
65.809539°N 39.101520°W @ 2,999 feet elevation

Eastern Greenland Ice cap

    Fabulously beautiful flight here. We were dropped off ~7pm. Flat ice and snow to the horizon ahead of us. Clumsy first night sleep chores but we'll get it. Need sleep. Cold is setting in.

Cold Arctic sunset for the first night of the expedition.

Day 0 (Aaron)
Friday, April 21, 2023
DYE-2: 206.6 miles, 286°

Terry and I caught our helicopter ride to the ice plateau at 6:15pm, very late. It was the only helicopter slot we could come up with. We had to pay to keep the airport open. At least we were able to arrange a flight at all.

The helicopter ride was incredible. The views were stunning. Wow! On a Bell 202 (?), one of the last flights for this chopper.

There is so much ice in the water. After a half-hour flight, the pilot touched down at the exact GPS coordinates we wanted. They sure don't want to fly one more minute. At $5,000USD, for the half hour there and paying for the half hour back, they really were exact. Though, the pilot asked if it was okay if he dropped us farther north since there was a possible cloud bank and whiteout. We said yes, but lucked out. No clouds.

When the pilot touch down, he raised and lowered the chopper several times, hitting the skids into the ice. This was the pilot's method of finding hidden crevasses while being able to escape unscathed.

We were dropped off, took our pictures, and the chopper was gone from the sky in minutes. We were blessed with perfect weather, a rare thing according to the pilot, and staked out camp at 7pm. Terry and I had to dig into our dinner, eating one of our day's meals. I'd not planned for that. I always get food at the airport but there wasn't anything for us there. Hopefully that doesn't catch up with us later.

We got ourselves into bed by 930pm which was good. We planned to wake up at 6am to take advantage of the cooler air.

It was getting dark. This march will be tougher because of the highly variable sun coverage. I wonder what the morning will be like. We both agreed that we'd need to shift our wakeup time to 4am in two days.

22 April, 2023 (Terry)
Camp 1
65° 51.265'N 39° 15.952'W
3,400 feet
5.6 miles from Camp 0

Rough 1st day today.

Beautiful weather, but tough ski conditions. Uphill, changing snow, very heavy sled. Stopped by the sled sticking not just dozens of times but hundreds! Aaron skied part way up the hill that I simply couldn't move the sled up. We stopped early and made camp. We are hoping to shift to skin earlier—maybe wake up at 4 a.m., ski as soon as ready (~7am) and get 6 shifts in by 4 p.m. Conditions need to ease or it will be a real battle to move it.

At our first stop for water and snacks, we were visited by an Arctic ptarmigan. He just walked around us only ~20 feet away. Pretty.

Terry smiles before skiing his first day in the Arctic.

Day 1 (Aaron)
Saturday, April 22, 2023

We had a great half-day of skiing, then started falling apart on a steep side slope. Our starting position should have been farther north. Terry had little trouble but the side slope really killed my feet. The surface was hard. I crashed once.

There was a bright spot to our first hard day—a ptarmigan visited us once we reached a plateau of sorts. We enjoyed this gentle bird's company for a little bit as we struggled our way up.

The day started cold and super windy, at least 30 knots, with little sun. Later, the day heated up. I really struggled. Terry did fine in the heat. I had no trouble in the super cold but Terry seemed to have a tough time with it. The cold breeze made it easy to power up and really push things along.

Terry struggled with his sled the whole day. He had trouble with the harness and rope position. I could see he was having trouble but he soldiered through it without a complaint. I was impressed.

We had fun until the last hot side hill, and then we both stumbled a bunch. I fell very hard once. There were many blue ice patches, so another hard fall could be a sprain or worse. In the evening, there was a rainbow ring around the sun. Bad weather on the way.

We found some soft snow and made a nice camp plateau on the otherwise steep hill. As soon as Terry measured our short 6 miles of travel, the weather calmed down. The workload felt like 10 miles but the surface was super steep.

Since we were having a tough time, we agreed to a 4 p.m. stop instead of 6 p.m. It wasn't ideal but we didn't want to get hurt, either. We'll wake up earlier to make up for it.

I pulled out the shotgun and had it ready on our gear in case of polar bears. There was a decent risk of running into one on the east side.

My ears were ringing. Why I was stressed? I knew that 6 miles a day wasn't going to cut it, especially when it felt that tough. I'm sure it'll get better but starting these trips is super tough.

Sunday, 23 April, 2023 (Terry)
Camp 2
65° 52.782' 39° 26.307' @ 4,168 feet
5.2 miles from camp 1

Felt great to stop & camp at 4 p.m. instead of 6 p.m.

Another tough day today. Weird blew last night pretty hard, but we stayed cozy. But the morning wind made breaking camp chaotic.

Skiing away from camp was nearly impossible on skis, so we switched to crampons. I immediately broke a strap. Repaired with paracord and we were on our way. But, we lost nearly a complete ski shift. Steady climbing & up lots of sastrugi to make it harder. Aaron switched back to skis before me. At first, I could keep up, but became knackered & wanted to quit early.

Every obstacle took all my strength to get the sled going again.

Aaron convinced me to get back on my skis for the night shift of the day, and he was right! I still had obstacles that stopped the sled & I had to muscle it over them, but overall I felt like I was expending less energy.

We woke a little after 4 a.m. and got skiing at 7 a.m. I should give us better light conditions & snow conditions.

Time for bed & a much-needed rest. Only made ~5.2 miles today, but climbed ~700 feet in poor conditions. We'll get better as conditions improve and we trail harden. The low overcast cleared this evening & the sky is blue.

We've left the coastal mountains behind & there is nothing but white stretching to the horizon in every direction.

Day 2 (Aaron)
Sunday, April 23, 2023

We woke up to blasting wind at 40 knots. Whoa. What a morning. Terry hadn't experienced this before, so I made sure to guide him in camp mechanics and preventing frostbite. It was good we had practiced this in 2018 and in 2019. As we prepped to strike camp, I asked Terry to communicate as much as possible. We wanted to make no mistakes. A lost glove, frostbite, or lost tent could be lethal.

The wind made things a bit rough but it was exciting for us this morning. We opted to use the vestibule for poop duty. Terry and I did the duty outside yesterday but today was impossible. Getting frostbite down there wasn't something we relished.

We started skiing at 7:10 a.m. which was great. 3 hours from waking to skiing. But, we were skiing blind in a white out. The surface was hard and slippery. Both our skis kept slipping. It was bad.

Terry convinced me to switch to crampons for this climb. At least we had grip and didn't slide around. It was super tough walking and feeling every undulation. Energy sucking, really. But at least we were able to climb the first serious hill. It was crazy steep.

Eventually, the ground leveled out and I switched back to skis. It was instant nirvana! When putting on his crampons, Terry's rubber crampon strap tore. He was a master, as he had his paracord out and cut a piece to lash the crampon onto his boot in no time. I was thoroughly impressed.

By 2 p.m., he was suffering pretty bad. "I'm knackered," he said. Walking through knee-deep snow in crampons towing a sled sinking into the mushy snow was rough.

It took a while of gentle convincing but he got back on his skis. The bad time from yesterday and this morning really worked him, so I had to convey that cramponing across Greenland wasn't possible. After some debating, he switched to skis.

In a short time, he perked up. We covered an entire other mile without being destroyed. By 3 p.m., the snow was soft and very sticky. Tough going. It was also 100% whiteout. I counted steps for navigation, walking 60 steps and then looking at my compass. The new Suunto

Terry realizes how vast the Greenland ice sheet is.

Terry finishes making camp after a long day.

compasses are terrible in this temperature. The needles stick badly.

Terry led one shift of 75 minutes. He did great. It was impressive to watch him forge into a whiteout. I took over to give him relief. The stress was clear on his face, knowing he had to keep us going.

I carried the shotgun and Terry's crampons to lighten his load. His emotional state improved. He's a chipper guy but the extra weight, whiteout, plus deep snow was taking a toll on him.

We camped at 4:10 p.m. after I added 100 yards to the day to save us later. It will pay off, I'm sure.

It took us nearly four hours from stopping to going to sleep rather than the usual 3.5 hours. We'll have to work on our efficiency a lot. We're both having a great time. What a challenge.

The top of my left knee hurts when I kneel and there's a slight burning sensation. Hopefully it doesn't turn into anything serious. Uh oh!

Aaron thinking about the length of the journey ahead.

Monday, 24 April, 2023 (Terry)
Camp 3
65° 54.345'N 39° 42.805' @ 4,534 feet
8 miles from Camp 2, 18.8 Total miles

Woke up to a whiteout snowstorm, our wind wall worked great!

By the time we broke camp & started moving, there was some blue sky, and by 11 a.m. the wind became very calm, then it got HOT. Temperature management is tough in these conditions.

Stopped a bit early (1530) because of foot hotspots (Aaron had a blister), probably because we were so hot and sweaty. Disappointed we didn't make better mileage, but we did climb significantly (370'). Thinking of 03:00 wakeup instead of 0:400 to avoid some of the afternoon heat. We hope to hit double digits in daily mileage.

Remember Robert of The Red House's crossings, one round trip, one of the widest points in 12 days with dogs. Wow!

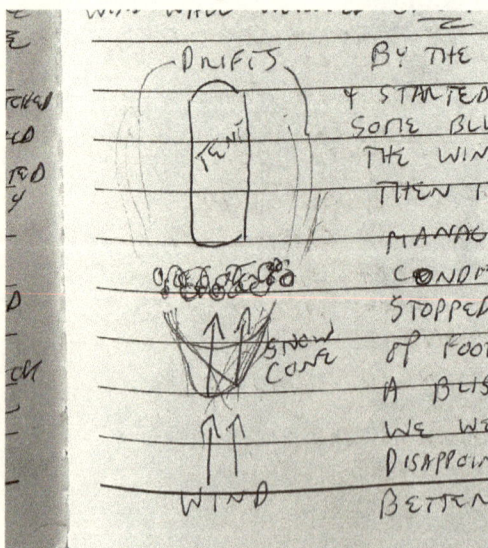

Wind wall design.

Day 3 (Aaron)
Monday, April 24, 2023

It started out quite windy and cold this morning, ending with us cooking and sweaty. I developed a small blister on the instep heel of my left foot. I've never gotten a blister there, so that was a unique experience.

We only did 8.0 miles!! Fudge! I was hoping to hit 12 miles. The sticky surface in the afternoon is just killing our daily distance. We'll get up at 3:15 a.m. tomorrow. The heat is just dragging us down.

We added 33% to our miles but we need another 25% on top of that. We're doing the 75-minute and 13 to 15-minute rest breaks. The temperature swing is just too dramatic.

I'll end up having to stop and change otherwise. I'll just have to start much colder and deal with it during each skiing shift.

After 2 p.m., the snow starts to melt and our speed plummeted.

I remember reading that other teams struggled to figure out how to adapt to the freeze and fry problem. Travel is easy when it's cold. But, our speed drops to half when it's hot. I broiled last night until 1 a.m., it was so hot. Then, I had to put my fleece jacket on. It's crazy warm compared to Antarctica when the sun hits daily.

We had a fun day—Terry is such a joy to trek with. I'm super glad and blessed to have him as an expedition partner.

We also gained 400 feet, that's a decent climb, too. We're at 4,584 feet. Climbing 400 feet adds at least an hour off of sled travel. We're holding on a bearing of 283° to reach DYE-2.

Terry led two shifts and did a great job. It was nice to follow. I needed to adjust his compass angle, otherwise, we ended up with a 20° error. I learned the same thing in Antarctica. These compasses are way too touchy.

Tuesday, 25 April, 2023 (Terry)
Camp 4, East Greenland Ice cap
65° 58.950'N 39° 56.878'W @ 5,100 feet
8.5 miles from camp 3
27.3 total miles

3 a.m. wakeup today so that we could ski earlier and avoid the afternoon heat and poor snow conditions. Very cold and windy as we left camp—Aaron was shivering & had cold fingers.

Started in tough sastrugi for me, but Aaron could blow through most of them. To help me, he took all the leads so that I could concentrate on getting over the obstacles. I'd see him hang up a little, then I'd make a strong run at it, success 50/50.

Had a change to much nicer snow conditions 1/2 through our 3rd shift, but by the 5th shift, it was getting hot & the snow was sticky, so a tough finish to the day. Clear blue sky. It feels like it will be a very cold night.

Overall, happy & encouraged to be making this many miles while climbing. As we get up onto the plateau more, hopefully, we can start making our mileage gains.

Terry melting snow for water and dinner.

Day 4 (Aaron)
Tuesday, April 25, 2023

Sleep was good at camp 3 but we woke up to 40-plus knot winds at 3 a.m.. Wow it was cold! There was frost in the tent for the first time.

We got out skiing by 6 a.m. It was pretty good considering the danger level. We hid behind the snow wall to get ourselves ready.

I made a big mistake by going too light on clothing. I went with just my wind pants with polar thigh guards, shell pants, a light shirt, my shell, and wintergreen parka only. I almost frostbit my right toes.

My air mat deflated three times last night. There must be a fiber or feather in the inlet/outlet cap. I've had this happen before.

I was on the absolute edge of freezing from 6 a.m. until 10 a.m. That was bad. I was violently shivering during towing. That's pretty bad. It also caused me to veer way off course when navigating.

I stopped for Terry to catch up while he struggled through the 1.5-foot tall sastrugi field. It was very tough going for him being so much lighter. He's putting on a good effort but it's just a physics problem.

I took the gun again to lower his weight. I already had the tent. I didn't notice the eight more pounds. It might be mental?

We enjoyed deep soft snow for hours in the afternoon. Fun! We camped on a hill at 5,000 feet, covering 8.5 miles again!

I had a delirium day where I was way off on my compass course, adding 1/3 mile of useless lateral travel. That cold made me go crazy.

Then, I overheated in the afternoon. I ended up doing this pathetic penguin walk to keep going. Terry complimented me on being a, "Big strong guy who shouldn't have any problem with this." I can do quite well, that is until I'm too hot. It'd literally be better to be -30°F all day.

Wednesday, 26 April, 2023 (Terry)
Camp 5, Ice cap
66° 01.207'N 40° 11.695'W @ 5,456 feet
7.4 miles from camp 4
Total distance 34.7 miles

Cold all night—I'm going to bed with much more clothing! Didn't sleep well again. Cold, windy start ~0630 (awake ~0330).

Aaron led first 2 ski shifts, but then conditions became softer & he was tired, so I led the next 2.5 shifts. Lots of snow made I slow going.

Crossed a set of POLAR BEAR TRACKS during the 3rd shift of skiing, only a couple of miles from camp. Not very filled in, so likely went by this morning sometime, at most yesterday. Tracks were heading south toward the coast in a pretty straight line.

Since then, whoever the skier behind has regularly scanned the horizon for the bear. No sightings yet, but were motivated to keep watch.

Again disappointed by the mileage, hopefully, we'll reach firm easier conditions soon. We can't make it across at this pace.

Evening chores done, in bed by ~2030.

Polar bear tracks over 60 miles (96 km) from the coast.

Day 5 (Aaron)
Wednesday, April 26, 2023

Another cold morning! My air mat continues to deflate through the fill valve. I'll keep cleaning it. I relieved myself twice, filling the bottle each time. This left me completely parched when I woke up. Now several of my fingers are split for not staying well hydrated in the evening.

We woke up at 3:20 a.m., 20 minutes late. This got us going by 6:40 a.m.

At mid-day, Terry led in the mushy show. I'm dragging pretty bad from the overheating yesterday.

We crossed fresh polar bear tracks!! They went north-south, though we couldn't tell which direction. Due to the wind, the bear likely walked by just a few hours before we arrived. Talk about a close call. It might see or smell us on the horizon.

Terry said, "Well, you wanted adventure!" Hahah, funny. Oops, be careful what one asks for.

At least the wind has been to our right at 3 o'clock. It burns the right side of our faces a bit but it's not like a headwind.

I was so fatigued yesterday, I could barely hold the 2-liter pot. I felt so weak including today.

Camp 5!

Crud! We only traveled 7.4 miles today. That's only 34 miles in 5 days. Ouch. The soft snow isn't helping our case. Amazingly steep hills make things tough and the sastrugi is really crushing Terry. Plus, I'm lagging badly from yesterday's heat exhaustion.

DYE-2 is 173 miles away. This soft snow is wrecking us. It firmed up today but still creates a huge lag.

Thursday, April 27, 2023 (Terry)
Camp 6, Greenland Ice cap
66° 03.084'N 40° 27.601'W @ 5,810 feet
7.8 miles from camp 5
Total distance 42.5 total miles

Moderate wind but very cold this morning. Maybe -10°F. Took us longer to get going, ~0645. Used mittens over liner gloves, but still had several long periods of frozen numbness & finally painful vasodilation. No skin damage visible, but some fingertips still numb. Also had some brief freezing on my upwind (right) check & nose, but just need to be careful. May try adhesive cheek pads and pole pogies tomorrow.

Snow conditions improved after ~3 shifts and the climbing gradient lessened.

Aaron bailed out of his leads several times, tired & blames it on the last couple of hot afternoons & poor sleep last night.

My pad deflated about midnight & the cold ice under my foam pack woke me up, so I had to re-inflate it. Very discouraging if that keeps happening. I haven't had a good night's rest yet.

So, between shifts 5 & 6, I challenged Aaron & said the snow conditions aren't that terrible. It's staying cold, so the sled is only sinking 2–3" inches. Aaron has been doing this "penguin walk" after he leads for only 10 minutes, where he started to take steps of 4 inches & slowed to less than 1/2 mile per hour. I told him that with these conditions, we should be able to stride out & rest in some miles. This just isn't the strong Aaron I know, so I hope he's okay. He seems more optimistic in the tent. We're sacked out at 1945, so hope some rest will help us recover.

Day 6 (Aaron)
Thursday, April 27, 2023

Colder and colder it becomes! It took us 3.5 hours from waking to skiing. We need to work on that. I had a FREAK OUT last night, waking up at 1:30 a.m., I panicked like I needed to run screaming out of the tent. After my heart stopped racing, I realized I had stopped breathing. My pulse was beating so strong I could feel my pulse on my forehead. Wow!

Terry's mat deflated last night. It has the same style valve as mine. Probably has fibers in the valve somewhere. Design weakness.

We made 7.8 miles today! In this soft snow, that's the best we can hope for. I so appreciated Terry saying, "You're a big strong man." That was such a boost. Even though it's a real worry that I'm failing. I can't ever remember someone giving me a compliment. He is super supportive—he is such a great friend. He's still breaking trail since I'm still fatigued from my heat exhaustion. He gave me an inner strength I didn't know I had.

He's really worried I'm falling apart but I will recover. I have had this happen before. I failed to eat my almonds, missing the salt. I felt it in my legs, the flutters of leg cramps, likely from the heat exhaustion 2 days ago.

I kept falling asleep skiing. Hahah. I'll bet Terry does fall asleep when he's following me.

We made camp at 3:30 p.m. and were asleep by 7:30 p.m. Last night we were up until 8:30pm, way too late.

We are still on schedule if all holds well. This was the first day I really smiled. This is serious but I still need to have fun.

Tomorrow, I'll put on my insulated gaiters. My feet have been too cold. Mom's custom gaiters make a big difference.

Terry is struggling badly with finger warmth. Hopefully he doesn't get a cold injury.

Friday, April 28, 2023 (Terry)
Camp 7
66° 05.118'N 40° 43.409'W @ 6,145'
7.8 miles from camp 6
50.3 miles total

Woke up to another cold, windy clear morning. Aaron thinks it's been -10°F the last few nights. (Cold enough to freeze my pee bottle solid—I won't do that again.) Used pogies & my hands did butter but they are a hassle.

Shift 1 - Aaron led strong in the cold unconsolidated snow (that he hates & has called such during hot afternoons up here"

Shift 2 - Lots of icy sastrugi. Very discouraging because I kept getting stopped & we weren't moving. Aaron offered to step in for a while & then I finished my lead when conditions improved.

Shift 3 - Cold unconsolidated snow. My lead & felt strong.

Shift 4 - Ditto for Aaron. He kept going even though he hates these conditions.

Shift 5 - My lead. Climbing in good conditions. Fatigued but okay. Blisters on left foot sole.

Shift 6 - Aaron finished off the day both tired & ready for bed.

In camp at 1530. Build a wind wall (always), tent up. Foot care for me then melting snow.

Bed ~1930. My inflatable mat leaked the last 2 nights. Hopefully not again, lips very sore. Sun? Cold? Wind? All 3.

Make up my bed counting on mat deflation. Foam pad, Aaron's & my shells & parks, inflatable/deflatable, sleeping bag. I wiped the pad valve and tried to remove down fuzz with no success.

Day 7 (Aaron)
Friday, April 28, 2023

Brr. It was even colder this morning with more frost in the tent. It was 3:10 a.m. for our wakeup time. We did pretty well, starting to ski by 630 a.m. We have to be very careful and methodical about the tent in the wind. It was blasting.

My fingers were on fire, though my toes were warmer from Mom's custom gaiters. Thank you Mom!

I wore my liners and alpine gloves. They're not good enough against that wind. I need my pogies or just buck up to my mittens.

We traveled 7.7 miles up to 6,000 feet, climbing 200 feet today.

Terry got emotionally crushed by sastrugi in shift 2. He's getting discouraged by the difficulty. I saw him stop and drop his shoulders and head. I gave him lots of encouragement.

I was able to put in 3.5 shifts today. I felt better after being crushed two full days from heat exhaustion fatigue. I learned to lie down and take a 10-minute nap while I was melting snow. That really helped.

I figured out that Greenland is 330 miles across in 30 days while the South Pole is 60 miles and about 40 days. The snow in Greenland is constantly sticky while the snow in Antarctica is hard and powdery. Greenland is twice as difficult as Antarctica in ski surface.

It's really breezy tonight. We had a cloud free day and it was cold tonight. We pray that the wind is more gentle tomorrow but still present to cool us.

Terry's name is Powder Master and I am Sastrugi Smasher. He does great grinding through the mushy powder. I don't like it at all. I am in my best in the worst conditions over the toughest sastrugi Terry said. He noted that the worse things were, the better I performed. Especially in white out, super windy conditions. We got to sleep at 730 p.m.

Saturday, 29 April, 2023 (Terry)
Camp 8
66° 07.045'N 40° 59.984'W @ 6,449' elevation
8.1 miles from camp 7
85.4 miles total
149.6 miles to DYE-2

Woke & started dressing at 03:00, but racing outside—40MPH winds & gusts to 50MPH. Maybe -10°F. Dangerous conditions, so we decided to sleep until 4 a.m., then get ready. So later start, 07:30.

Session 1: Raging, lots of sastrugi. Aaron led strong. Used posies to save hands.

Session 2: I asked Aaron to keep leading because of the sastrugi. Glasses still iced up, couldn't see after ~10 minutes, good snow so I took my lead.

Session 3: Aaron. Improving conditions. Strong lead, my friend is back!

Session 4: Warmer, winds light. I lead over goo snow & not too difficult sastrugi.

Session 5: Aaron. Talked about being too hot, but really just overdressed.

Session 6: Me. Fatigued but okay. Raw foot where I have 2 blisters.

Made camp in calm winds. Will stick with a 4 a.m. wakeup tomorrow.

I've been working on correcting some ski mechanics. When I tire, I tend to roll the right ankle. Happened lots 3 days ago & that's what caused my blisters.

Aaron noticed me stretching my shoulder an offered that my soreness was the way I hold my poles with mittens on. Always the engineer trying to fix things… I answered that it's fatigue.

Day 8 (Aaron)
Saturday, April 29, 2023

Up at 3 a.m.

It's storming baby! Stormin Norman à la General Schwarzkopf. The wind was ripping up to 50 knots, pushing snow six feet or more into the air. This is the max we could handle, so we decided to tough it out and travel. I was proud of Terry for facing the danger.

I wore all of had for a bit, then I was too hot all day. The weather variability here is mind-blowing. Haha!

The storm calmed down by noon and it was nice. We chose to wake up at 4 a.m. to avoid the storm frostbite. We cracked 8 miles today! Woo hoo! Thank you God!

I remodeled Dad and Mom's house some more in my mind. I added ideas to my place, too. I received a text message from Kelly. She's so great. I hope they're not worried about us at home.

It's late and I must rest. Sleep.

Aaron in full storm armor.

Sunday, 30 April, 2023 (Terry)
Camp 9
66° 08.645'N 41° 16.509'W @ 6,692 feet
7.9 miles from camp 8
66.3 miles total
141 miles from DYE-2

Up too late. Bed at 2130 and poor sleep. Mat continued to fail.
A day of extremes. Biting cold but mild wind as we woke up.
Late start, 07:45 a.m. — struggled in the cold.
I took the first shift. Felt good to be out. Super cold snow and air.
Accidentally spilled my drink on the sled bag at first break. Froze immediately. The temperature Aaron thinks it is -25°F.

Second shift, Aaron led out strong
3rd shift - Me, mixed snow conditions but improved. Felt like we covered good ground in the last 3 shifts.
4th - Aaron. Lead strong.
5th - Wind dying down. Hot, sore feet, Aaron took over for the last 10 minutes or so because I was slowing.
6th Aaron. Now, no wind, amazingly hot feeling. We both stripped to base layers and shirts not to flame out.

At camp, still amazingly hot as we set up. Doctored my feet after unloading into the tent. Just a blister in a bad spot. Melting water now. Slight breeze came up to show us how cold the air actually is. Well below freezing, probably 0°F.

The math doesn't really work for us finishing on time but Aaron is optimistic. Once we hit better conditions and ski downhill with lighter sleds, we can do it. I love the optimism.

Day 9 (Aaron)
Sunday, April 30, 2023

Brr, it's -25°F to -30°F this morning. We're up by 4 a.m. and skiing by 7:45 a.m. It was a very late start. This delay put us into bad heat with no wind after 2 p.m. But, the hard surfaces were great. We were thankful to have covered 7.9 miles!

We climbed a good 300 feet, getting toasted in the last two ski shifts. It was hot and there was no breeze. This eastern side is rough.

I learned Terry has sweaty feet syndrome, so his feet blistered. I did notice in the first three days that his ski technique caused his right foot to sink and angle to the right. I asked him about it and he said that was his normal gait. Hopefully those blisters aren't painful, but I suspect they are. Probably like walking on broken glass.

We lost a mile to heat fatigue. It was a completely windless evening, dead silent. I had Terry yell. He said it was surreal to hear no reflection, as though we were in space. I love it. We're praying for a hard surface and faster travel tomorrow.

It was a good day, climbing to 6,6667 feet. We camped at 4:14 p.m. and were in sleeping bags by 8 p.m. Thank you Lord for comfortable conditions.

Windy morning in the Arctic.

Monday, 1 May, 2023 (Terry)
Camp 10
66° 11.402'N 41° 33.223'W @ 6,950 feet
8.4 miles from camp 9
Total 74.7 miles
DYE-2 is 133.4 miles away

Slept poorly again. Inflatable sleep pad again failed. (Started ~ Camp 6?). Tricks to stay warm when it deflates.

Cold morning and moderate to light wind. Started ~0630 (moved wakeup time to 0300 to avoid hot afternoon when the wind dies).

1st shift - I tried to lead, but Aaron took over because I was moving slow. Lots of friction in the sled, and glasses iced, so I was blind. Strong lead by Aaron!

2nd shift - Again Aaron, very strong-kept us moving despite hard conditions. At break, I spilled my drink on sled, instantly froze on sled bag. Aaron says wind chill -45°F.

3rd shift - I led and worked hard to keep us moving well & spare Aaron. Climbing most of the shift, then eased.

4th shift - We both needed to recover, so Aaron led at an easier pace.

5th shift - I lead. Air crisp and cold, but wind dying down, so we both shed layers to avoid overheating.

6th shift - Light wind kept us from overheating. Like the last several afternoons, it's nice to finish at 1530.

At camp, I needed to re-dress blisters on my left foot because the old dressings shifted and came off. Will feel better when it's healed.

Had trouble tonight with finishing the large portion of cashew curry. Just not my fav. But last night's pesto pasta & salmon—yum!

On track to being in bed by 715pm. I could use some extra rest.

Aaron is optimistic now—feels if we can make it to DYE-2 in 20 days, we should make it. It will be downhill, sleds will be lighter, etc. We just can't have storm days!

Daydreams today about long hot tub soaks, holding Diane.

Day 10 (Aaron)
Monday, May 1, 2023

We woke up at 315 a.m. and were skiing at 8 a.m. Traveled 8.4 miles. Woo hoo! I absolutely froze this morning but I had to wear thin long underwear and my thin shirt to be able to survive the mid-day heat.

Terry's glasses kept fogging up in the morning, so I took the first and second shift lead. Normally we switched off but with his fogged glasses, navigation was impossible for him. I don't think he realized he was going to ski across Greenland half-blind. I was used to it.

I also took the shotgun again to balance our speed. It's pointless if I'm faster or riding on his tail.

The wind made me shiver badly, this was normal on breaks. It's annoying but I knew it'd happen. Terry is doing better. He handles the heat far better, so he can bundle up and not overheat during the day.

I need my pogies to protect my hands but I failed to add Velcro to my parka like my Mom suggested 10 years prior. Always listen to your mom.

The third shift was better. Terry took us up on a climb to 7,000 feet! The fourth shift was good, we shed layers. We skied from 630am to 330pm.

I apologized to Terry for suggesting that making himself much colder would prevent his sweaty feet. I didn't know he had a syndrome that makes his feet sweat even when he is cold and it's sub-zero. (I wrote this yesterday but am emphasizing it today). Better to clear the air. Sorry Terry!

I have a book idea (what's new?). I can write a book on 100+ tips on cold weather camping with adventure tips. I'll add my little tidbits from this journal, Antarctica, and my YouTube channel.

Terry's book idea is to write a book about friendship wrapped in this Greenland adventure. What a great idea! He'll write it and I'll add my material, then he'll present it at his church in fall. I think his idea is much better than mine.

We climbed an additional 300 feet today. The summit is about 70 miles away. This endless climb has to flatten out eventually, as the summit plateau is theoretically at 8,100 feet. Soon we'll stop the big altitude gains and pick up more miles.

Tuesday, 2 May, 2023 (Terry)
Camp 11
66° 13.594'N 41° 50.999'W @ 7,123 feet
Distance from Camp 10: 8.6 miles
Total 83.6 miles
125 miles to DYE-2, new bearing of 280°

Weird dreams about camping somewhere dangerous with Aaron, that some bad guys were after us. We were camping in Southern California chaparral in this dream.

Very cold start at 0630. Aaron thinks -30°F or so. Fortunately light winds or the wind chill would've been deadly.

I struggled today but Aaron was in his element! He led the first 3 sessions. Felt like pulling sleds through sand. Hard effort given. Aaron very strong.

4th session- I led, temperatures moderating, still very cold. I had to have a bowel movement. I only had 20 minutes in my shift, so it ruined my rhythm! I experienced the Arctic full Monty & snow bidet.

5th session - I was dragging. Aaron led again. Some sore feet as the moleskin failed on my foot blisters. I'll try Leukotape tonight.

6th session - we split. Very tired and dragging. Aaron tired but still moving strong. Extra 15 minutes to "Pay the Piper". (Did the same yesterday, we'll probably keep doing it to make up our deficit).

Better & more efficient at building wind wall. Dinner & rest needed.

Doctored feet with Leukotape, but had to warm it first. Aaron made a cup of hot water for tea while I did this—nice!

Inflatable mat still failing, using clothing under as extra insulation.

Light winds but very cold now. To bed at 1930.

All fingertips numb from ~day 3. Hard to know how much risk I'm putting my hands through with all these freeze/thaw cycles every morning. No skin changes of frostbite (yet).

Daydreams today—people on tour to Hill 660 offer to take us out to dinner to hear the story of our crossing. We order plates of pure food!

Day 11 (Aaron)
Tuesday, May 2, 2023

We started skiing at 630 a.m. I froze my left ring and thumb fingers. I don't know why they got cold, but the right-side wind cuts across. My fingers were dead numb, dead wood, so I stuck them in my crotch for a bit. Once the sensation came back, it was like fire.

We covered 8.6 miles. Woo hoo!

I was enjoying flirting with the first stages of frostbite. Crazy. I need to wear the mittens and triple socks. It's just too cold for how fast we can go to make heat versus fatiguing out.

Terry was cool but comfortable. What a dedicated husband—he said he was thinking about hot tubbing with his wife while we were battling against frost damage. Way to get hot!

My stomach skin even got cold prickles, from the 45–90° to the right wind. That means I'll be enjoying chilblains for the rest of the trip.

Wish I'd been smart and put Velcro on my parka to keep the pogies in place. I should just try the mittens. I don't want to use them unless it's extreme, but it's already extreme by freezing my fingers. The problem is with mittens, I can't do much. But frostbitting my fingers will be worse.

In the third shift, things smoothed out. We're still freezing, though. Terry had to enjoy his first outside bowel movement. Fun times!

In the last session, we enjoyed incredible conditions. The surface was hard and we had flat running. This was the best ever. By the end of the day, Terry sat tired on his sled. This was the first time he'd done that. Guess the fatigue of the expedition is catching up with him. He's tough.

It was super cold snow, so it was like towing the sleds in sand. The snow doesn't melt allowing for glide in temperatures below -25°F or lower.

I must wear triple socks and mittens tomorrow. Another set of stomach skin prickles. Prepare for damage.

We climbed 170 feet today. The last shift rocked. The temperature went up, the surface was hard, it was such a good feeling. We've not had that great a time in over a week.

We laid down at 730 p.m. and were asleep in minutes.

Wednesday, 3 May, 2023 (Terry)
Camp 12, Ice cap
66° 15.393'N 42° 08.619'W @ 7,417 feet
8.4 miles from camp 11
Total 92 miles
116 miles to DYE-2, bearing 279°
Climb to the Apex at 8,177 feet

Another very cold—we both put on extra layers on core & used pogies. About -25°F!

Fortunately mild winds. I cleaned two pounds of ice out of my sled.

Aaron led the first 2 shifts, very strong. He's in his element! Almost constant sastrugi, easier sled pulling than yesterday. 2nd shift I just couldn't match him, so he took the shotgun.

I led the 3rd shift, did okay. Blistered foot pretty comfortable. I was more careful with ski mechanics.

Aaron led the 4th shift somewhat slower now, it's uphill. Hard to tell.

5th shift I lead. Had to make clothing adjustments in the middle of the shift. The wind is easing and it makes it feel so much warmer.

6th shift - Again Aaron led. We both peeled down & I put on a boonie hat.

We rolled into camp & light wind. There's a bit of low clouds. Does this mean weather change?

Re-dressed blistered and doing evening chores. Always look forward to when we can lie down.

Both always hungry—I spend a lot of the ski shift thinking about what we'll eat next. Daydreamed a lot today about seeing my life group friends at a welcome home pot luck.

I dreamt I burst into tears on seeing them & having trouble telling them how much I missed & loved them. Also daydreamed about Diane picking me up at the airport, and how excited the puppies will be to see me.

Aaron continues to be always positive. What a great expedition partner. Mentioned today that this is A LOT more fun than solo.

Day 12 (Aaron)
Wednesday, May 3, 2023

It was cold but not as windy, thank the Lord! It was -25°F to -30°F. We put Terry in mittens and pogies. I helped him put on his last poggy since it was impossible for him to do. He lamented being dressed like a 2-year-old. I told him I didn't care, and I'd do it a dozen times a day if necessary. As long as he doesn't get frostbite and wreck his fingers, it's not a problem for me.

I went with my extra fleece vest to stay warm, wore the triple socks, and finally put on mittens. Wow what a difference! My feet aren't freezing. My toes did get cold at the end of the first shift but they were never on fire. This, I can handle. Terry's foam Intuition liners blow away my mashed wool liners. The problem is his feet are torching hot while mine stay cool in the afternoon. Blisters vs frozen feet.

My fingers were so warm, they were sweaty. Haha. Good ol' Outdoor Research Altimittens.

It was quite cold through shift four, we started at 645 a.m., waking up at 315am. It's amazing how starting 15 minutes later can throw off our whole day. We're quite efficient in the morning but battling the wind to save the tent and dig out is an uncontrolled variable.

We climbed nearly 400 feet to 7,417 feet! It's less than 800 feet of elevation gain to go.

It feels like the elves are dragging the sleds backward with ropes.

In theory, it's 40 miles to the Greenland summit at 8,177 feet according to the maps. DYE-2 is at 6,933 feet and 76 miles from the summit. Point 660 is at 1,268 feet. In theory, we only have 730 feet left to climb. Woo hoo!

Cooking in the vestibule during a storm.

Thursday, 4 May, 2023 (Terry)
Camp 13, Ice cap
66° 16.290'N 42° 28.893'W @ 7,664 feet
9.5 miles from Camp 12
Total 101.5 miles

Woke to unusually different weather pattern. It was almost a windless night, and 1–2 inches of new snow. I thought we'd start with poor visibility, but it cleared out quickly. It was pleasant skiing on cold now snow. It evened out the sastrugi.

As usual, Aaron started strong. He loves the cold.

We swapped leads all day. Heavier unconsolidated snow to go through late in the day. Surprised we got this many miles in.

We're behind, so Aaron wants to ski an extra 30 minutes per day instead of 15 minutes.

My feet are still very painful. I need them to heal so I can enjoy pushing harder.

My mind was blank all day. Tried hymns to get read of the "ear worms".

Daydreamed about being invited on "The Five" to talk about our Greenland book, and Diane and I get to go out to lunch with Dana & Peter Perino (sp?).

Skis perform well in this snow. We just need to get more miles each day. We're cutting it too close! Aaron keeps re-calculating the daunting mileage to finish. We'll start adding an additional 30 minutes of skiing to the end of the day.

Day 13 (Aaron)
Thursday, May 4, 2023

Good morning Greenland! It's a total whiteout and there's a decent breeze to keep us cool. When it's a whiteout, I lead the shifts. Terry doesn't feel confident wandering totally blind. After a few wanders, I get things lined up and we travel almost straight.

It ended up being a nice day with the breeze crossing from our right side. It's cold!

The GPS says we traveled 9.5 miles?! Wow, and we gained elevation to 7,728 feet! We were both really sore from the effort. My Achilles hurt from improperly tying my boots this morning. I pointed my toe while syncing up the laces to prevent heel lift which causes strain on the tendon. On top of that, I'm tearing through my wool boot liners.

One to two inches of snow fell last night. It felt like we slowed down, yet we gained more mileage otherwise. Smoother surface and less stoppages for shedding layers for heat. Each stop costs us a lot of distance, rather than shedding when we stop for breaks. Rookie move on my part, but we're still freezing. Then, when skiing, the temperature rockets and we don't have a choice but to stop.

The Greenland summit is still 42 miles away. Ugh! It's at 8,199 feet. 7,782 feet is our current elevation, so we only have 417 feet more climbing.

DYE-2 is 107 miles away. DYE-2 to Point 660 is another 112 miles. Total 219 miles yet to go. We have our pickup on 5/27. Today is 5/24. So we have 27–5 = 22 days to cover this whole trip. Whoa. We need to hit 9.9 miles per day to stay alive. That's with storm days included. We did 9.5 miles today, but still need 40 miles to the summit.

The schedule relies on us hitting the summit, then losing altitude and gaining speed to make it with zero storm days. Talk about cutting it close. We both agreed starting at the coast out of Isortoq would've been an epic mistake. We would've had to make up an extra shift. As was, by day 4, we were adding a half-hour shift realizing we weren't going to make it.

Terry said other expedition companies wrote they start out easy. What I pointed out as they never wrote that to make up for that, they'd have to do 7–8 shifts a day. Misery to make people feel better about

Terry skiing toward the edge of the Earth in Arctic oblivion.

it. Several blogs I read said they were doing 8 shifts, only sleeping 5 hours a night. To avoid that, we simply added a half hour a day. Over the whole expedition, that would subtract 3 days from or end (or so). It's the theory of Scott marching an additional 100 yards per day. That would've saved their lives.

When Terry is struggling with his hands (he got frostbite years ago on Shasta, so he has Raynaud's syndrome of easily frozen hands), I open my parka and give him shelter from the wind. I look like a flasher from the old New York days. It looks funny. It's easy for us to stitch our skis together, I put on his last pogie. Even then, it's so cold he's swirling around his arms, trying to keep blood flowing.

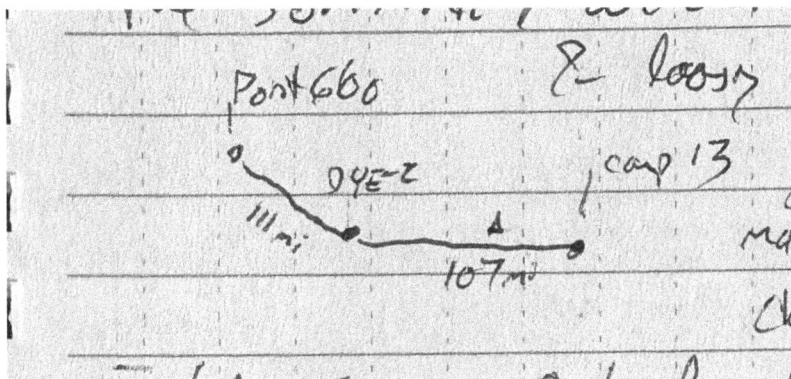

May 4 plotting of distances.

Enjoying cold granola cereal for an Arctic breakfast.

Friday, 5 May, 2023 (Terry)
Camp 14, Ice cap
66° 17.707'N 42° 48.987'W @ 7,845 feet
9.5 miles from camp 13
Total 111 miles
97 miles to DYE-2

Restful night, not much wind. Up at 3 a.m., skiing at 0600!

Very cold, so cold winds are a blessing. Aaron says it feels like -30°F.

We alternated leads. Aaron strong in the cold as usual. Lots of friction in the snow.

More comfortable temps by the 3rd session, so I took off the pogies. Never warm enough today for me to shed the ruff parka.

Feet still very sore, especially shifts 4–6 and the bonus 30-minute shift.

Brewing curry for supper now. Opening a new food bag is like Christmas!

Aaron mentioned in the tent that this trip is as hard as the temperatures and terrain in Antarctica.

This is the 10th anniversary of his Antarctic trip. He's glad to do both. Says this trip is, "No Joke."

At our second shift break, Aaron said, "There's nobody I'd rather be doing this with."

I replied that I felt the say way and felt lucky to be doing this with such a skilled and experienced polar traveler.

Got to bed at 1930. Hoping my feet heal soon.

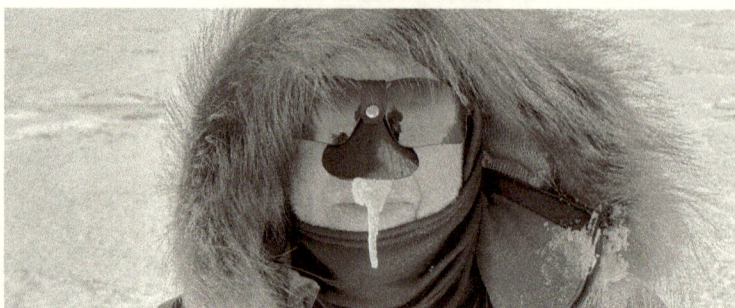

Terry is from southern California yet smiles despite the icicle on his nose.

Day 14 (Aaron)
Friday, May 5, 2023

It was an extremely cold morning but with light winds thank the Lord. My left hand, the downwind one since the wind comes from the right on the eastern side of the summit, got cold even in the Altimitts. Holding the ski poles is brutal, even with the cork handles. My Casio ProTrek watch face fogged, so it has to be at least -35°F, about the same temperature as the South Pole.

We gained altitude to 7,850 feet and covered 9.5 miles. Woo hoo, we're still alive.

The early snow was extremely sticky. It was just too cold. The hauling was tough. We didn't make any clothing changes because it was so cold. Terry went fast but is badly struggling because of his foot blister from the damage on day 3, over ten days ago.

His right foot ski technique of letting his right foot slide down and to the right wrecked his foot. He had me take a picture, thinking it was worse. It didn't look bad but he struggled bandaging, saying it was like broken glass. He did admit it was weak ski technique, not his body mechanics. I felt terrible for him. The constant pain must be mind-numbing. He sure keeps a positive attitude for the pain he's in.

We hit our first downhill!!! Oh my gosh, what a feeling it was to come over that crest and ski downhill. I took off at a race. I shouldn't have but it was too exciting.

In theory, the summit is 33 miles away. Soon we'll enjoy rolling hills and then some downhill. After two weeks of grinding endless uphill, we're nearly there. We'll get speed!

I thought about Dad all day. I remember him sitting with me on my bed with a football team logo bedspread, telling me about his first Boy Scout camping trip. He told me to be brave and that I'd have fun. It was one of the best memories I have with my Dad. I wonder if he remembers that moment?

I am here because of Dad (and Mom's) loving encouragement. I'm so blessed to have parents like these married 50 years ago!

Saturday, 6 May, 2023 (Terry)
Camp 15, Ice cap
66° 19.564'N 43° 12.889'W @ 8,034 feet
11.3 miles from camp 14
Total 122.3 miles
86.5 miles to DYE-2
[Wind shifted to southeast.]

Eventful day. Aaron asked me at 2 a.m. if we should get an earlier start. I reminded him of how "sticky" the snow often is that early, so we slept until 3 a.m. He suggested it because there's no wind. It was overcast and flat light when we got out to ski at 0545. Mild temperatures of ~0°F.

1st shift Aaron led. We crossed a sled track only 1–2 days old, heading in a more North-South direction. Aaron skiing fast & strong.

2nd shift I led off. It started to snow lightly, okay so far. Eventually deteriorated to "inside the ping pong ball." Conditions were very disorienting. I slowed so much that Aaron took over & led the rest of the shifts, keeping us moving fast. He wants to make the mileage we need.

A weak storm seemed to blow though, but the wind picked up and changed 180° from the usual. We had stripped off layers because we were skiing so hard, but had to armor up for the rest of the afternoon.

Cold winds blowing at our backs from the southeast (back left). Aaron had me lead for 25 minutes in the last shift so he could recover. We then did a 30-minute "bonus round" & did an additional mile! Great total for today. I couldn't keep up, but he's determined to keep us moving!

At camp, we built the best wind call yet & made extra protection for my windward vestibule. To keep us moving faster, Aaron has been hauling the shotgun. Now, he's got the first aid kit & the morning thermos also.

My feet are improving. I took the dressings off for the night so they can dry. We were in bed by 8 p.m.

Aaron & I talked about other strategies to move faster. He's willing to lead much more. I told him I didn't want to resent me for not pulling my weight. We slept great despite the wind noise in the tent. Must be exhaustion.

Our constant companions, cold, hunger, and exhaustion.

Day 15 (Aaron)
Saturday, May 6, 2023

We started skiing at 545 a.m.

DYE-2 is 86 miles away. It should be 8 days of travel. The summit is 22 miles, so it should be 2 days away. Point 660 is 194 miles away. At 11 miles per day, it should be 18 days away. That's going to be really close to our pickup date. Nothing like a little bit of stress.

Terry is a great speed manager. He's always fine-tuning where he puts on the power and where he holds back. It's probably smarter than me going at 80–85% all the time. It's a challenge to figure out the right balance.

He follows me at his 95% speed (since I'm faster), so when he leads, he's running at a 70% power rate according to him. For the first 20 minutes, I'm slower than him, recovering from my shift. But by the end, I'm tailing pretty close. It's a tough balance.

I swapped to near-freezing clothes and poured on the throttle today, covering 10.2 miles by 6 p.m. We added our 35 minutes ad got it to 11.3 miles.

I called it "paying the Piper." Getting that extra mile will pay off at the end of the trip.

Our schedule today was me on shift 1, Terry on 2, me on 3, Terry on 4. Once the sky went to whiteout in shift 4, he started going in circles and almost fell over while looking at his compass. He was a good sport about it and enjoyed the experience. We learned that I was to take over when it was 100% whiteout. He did okay as long as he could see something.

I started getting cold burns on my face. A storm of wind and snow came up after a completely calm morning. We survived and built an extra-big snow wall. It was worth it.

We're 20 miles and 2 days from the summit. And then it should be all downhill!

We decided to have me lead for speed and Terry lead to let me recover.

Both Terry and my lips are DESTROYED. They hurt so bad I couldn't hardly sleep last night.

Sunday, 7 May, 2023 (Terry)
Camp 16, Ice cap
66° 20.044'N 43° 35.741'W @ 8,222 feet
10.6 miles from camp 15
Total 132.9 miles
75.7 miles to DYE-2, 184 miles to Hill 660

Aaron proclaims this is "Greenland National Tar Pit Day" because of slogging uphill through sticky snow.

Shift 1 - Aaron lead, climbing and fine
Shift 2 - I took 2nd half to let Aaron recover
Shift 3 - I lead, changing light conditions with "diamonds in the sky"
Shift 4 - Aaron led, pretty flat light, some snow blowing
Shift 5 & 6 - We split up to make less arduous
Shift bonus - Aaron led both of us knackered

Moderate winds all night, with a cold morning. Maybe -10°F. Light snow. Very tough navigational conditions. We started skiing 0600. The new dressings on my feet felt good for the first 3 shifts.

The new wind pattern continues, at our backs out of the southeast.

Changing light & gently blowing snow was very pretty.

During the flat light sessions, Aaron led. I tried to help & navigate, but Aaron asked me to hold it unless he veered way off. The small corrections interfered with his concentration and system. Good communication & I get it.

Daydreams about speaking on this expedition at the Southern California Kaiser Fall Celebration Dinner. Some new ideas for the book.

The tent was warmed by the sun when we went to bed. It was too warm at first for good sleep.

We got to bed about 2000.

Day 16 (Aaron)
Sunday, May 7, 2023

Woo! 10.6 miles The summit is 12.2 miles away. Point 660 is 184 miles away. If all goes well, it'll be there in 18 days, May 26, if we can pick up some speed, even earlier. DYE-2 is 75 miles away, about 7.5 days.

I took the first shift in the 100% whiteout. This time, I didn't have Terry give me corrections unless I was way off course for a long time. I learned it was tough to take the feedback while skiing blind. Terry was a good sport about it and didn't take it badly at all.

There was a killer hill climb in shift 2 with soft wind slabs. Terry suggested I try much longer strides than short steps. WOW—what a difference! I couldn't believe I covered more distance with the same amount of energy. Guess that's why he's the doctor.

My front lower teeth are now very cold-sensitive. Probably from the aching lips.

The new Chili Mac from Mountain House isn't that good. It smells like cheap beef.

Terry felt dismayed we wouldn't make it, that we're not covering the miles. It's super tight but we're still alive. He called it Camp Disappointment.

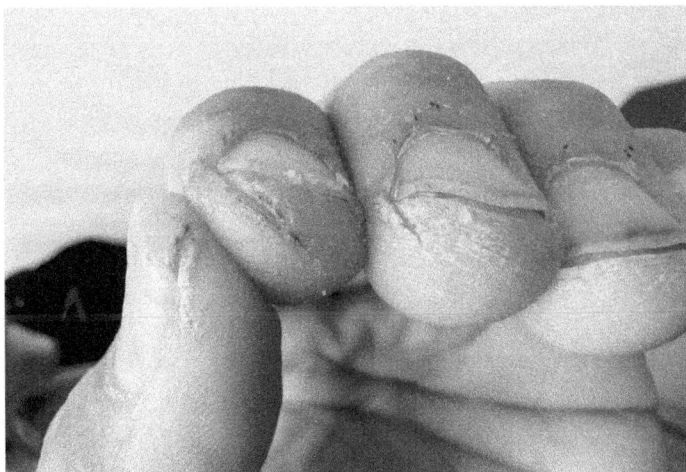

Split finger tips makes touching anything feel like a needle stab every time.

Monday, 8 May, 2023 (Terry)
Camp 17, Ice cap
Summit Camp
66° 22.242'N 44° 00.195'W @ 8,100 feet elevation
11.6 miles from camp 16
Total 144.5 miles

We started skiing at 0620. Moderate winds during the night died down & we woke to calm winds, dusting snow, and solid overcast. But you could see the sun & horizon.

When we set out, the light was very flat and it was -10°F.

Aaron led off and reminded me he didn't want navigational feedback unless he was way off.

Slow session 1 - Felt like we climbed some or is Aaron still tired from push 2 days ago?

Session 2 - I lead. Light improved & did okay navigating. I set a fast pace & it felt good. Did 1/2 hour of downhill. Felt really good!

Session 3 - Aaron lead. Improved surface & light. I saw 2 skiers about 1 mile south of us, crossing to the east. I took pictures.

[OTHER SKIERS GOING EAST]

Session 4 - I lead. Cool wind at our backs out of the SE seems to be normal now. Kept us from having to change.

Session 5 - Aaron lead. Good steady pace.

Session 6 - I led. Feet sore but okay.

Bonus session - Aaron led to summit camp.

As we skied, the wind freshened from the southeast. Fog and overcast 360° on the horizon with blue sky overhead. God's provision for us?

By the time we made camp, the sky was beautiful and we did summit photos.

Happy about daily mileage. 3 days in a row of double digits. Keep this up & we might make it!

Day 17 (Aaron)
Monday, May 8, 2023

I woke up at 1:30 a.m. and couldn't get back to sleep. I must've worried I was missing the 3 a.m. wakeup from my watch. Maybe I need a mechanical alarm clock.

The morning went well and we started skiing by 6:30 a.m. I took the first shift into the whiteout. Terry hands me that duty. I could 15 steps and then course correct. I used to do 60 steps but with the unreliable compass, that's too much. This keeps us skiing pretty well.

We started at 6:20 a.m. but I called it 630am for easy math. We did get hopefully our last hill in shift 3. We lost 120 feet of elevation today even though we're not at the Greenland summit. Woo hoo. That means we're cresting the hill.

Energy-wise, we are halfway there. We are also half-way through our days on the calendar. We did 11.6 miles today and did nothing crazy! Changing my stride and hitting rolling hills made such a difference. We've skied 144.5 miles so far. Nice.

I noticed some toe fungus on both of my small toes. Athlete's foot. Bummer. For some reason, I missed bringing the Tinactin.

Terry spotted two skiers south of us at the apex while he was doing his horizon polar bear scan. They were barely visible, falling in and out of the clouds and fog.

We are at the ice cap summit and halfway there whether we like it or not. We add a half-hour shift at the end of the day which buys us an additional day at the end. We are looking good barring a big storm or disaster. Please keep us safe!

Smiling while facing adversity makes the cold, aches, and discomfort melt away.

Pesto pasta & olive oil and salmon for dinner—a feast. My favorite. Wish I'd brought more of it.

Bed at 2000. Wind freshening. We still can't afford any storm delays. We are both feeling good but tired. Feet still sore but seem to be turning the corner.

Aaron said, "Have we climbed anything tougher than yesterday?"

I said, "Aaron, have you forgotten days 1, 2, 3, 4, 5, …?"

Daydreams today about being the spokesperson for the complete cookie. It's my favorite snack between ski sessions.

Eastbound ski team 1 mile (1.6 km) away.

Terry (left) and Aaron at the Greenland summit ~8,100 ft (2,469m).

Aaron's bleeding lips from ultraviolet light and extreme cold.

Tuesday, 9 May, 2023 (Terry)
Camp 18, Ice cap
66° 23.940'N 44° 25.647'W @ 7,915 elevation
11.9 miles from camp 17
Total of 156 miles

Awoke to light winds, milder temperatures at maybe +10°F. There was a light dusting of snow outside and rime frost on everything. We started skiing just before 0600.

It's a solid overcast & flat light, so Aaron led as usual when navigation is tough. There was an improved sliding surface for the pulks. We tried to set a sustainable pace. Both fatigued, trading leading ski sessions.

Session 2 - I led. Flat light, tough navigation. At one point, the sun suddenly lit me up. Aaron said it was spectacular but couldn't get his camera out in time.

Session 3 - Aaron Led.

Session 4, 5, 6 - We traded off. Navigating a huge area of sastrugi. It stayed cool until session 6 when I led and we both shed our parkas. Very light snowfall with a beautiful sky all day. Some snow squalls blew by.

I'm hoping for less fatiguing downhill conditions soon. We will drop about 20 feet per mile to DYE-2. Very happy to cover double-digit miles for the 5th day in a row. We might make it without storm delays.

Can you expect 25 straight days up here without storm delays?

Set up camp in light winds. Now, no wind at all! The last 3 nights, the sun was warmed up our tent to a comfy temperature. It was almost too hot for our bags. I mended my torn shell pants while melting snow.

A new blister developed on my right heel. When will my feet toughen up?

We hit bed by 1915. Aaron is already sleeping. He took 3 breaths and he was out. We're half-way time-wise and mileage-wise! Hopeful for less exertion pulling the pulks soon!

I need to remember to tell Diane that my favorite daydream is sitting next to her in the hot tub or the couch & listening to her talk and catch me up on things.

Day 18 (Aaron)
Tuesday, May 9, 2023

Our less-than-ideal starting location suggested we are done by day 32 given no storm days.

Camp 18—we made 11.9 miles! We encountered an unexpected hill. We felt it but couldn't see it. The slightest incline makes such a difference. The wind really died. The heat just roasted me.

There were 2.5 shifts of sastrugi patches to cross. They aren't large but they just didn't end. This patch was bigger than any other I've encountered.

This is where the wind started to shift, right after reaching the peak. Instead of off to the right, about 90°, the wind is very shifty at the apex, so the katabatic effect is swirling up here.

In 52 miles, we'll drop 1,000 feet, about 20 feet per mile. I hope soon.

Our drop-off point cost us 3 days of crawling. (I think). Starting farther north would've been much better. We're still okay without any delays.

Point 660 is 161 miles away. Today is day 18 + 16 days = 34 days. That's really too close for comfort. Adding an additional 30-minute shift will pay off at the end.

This particular sastrugi patch looks and feels like Antarctica. This is what I expected. But, this also means we're in a very strong wind region.

Terry tore the crotch in his shell pants. He used my sewing kit to make a repair. He was in business in 30 minutes.

I slept horribly last night, thrashing around. Who knows what is on my mind this time? Probably over-analyzing things.

Wednesday, 10 May, 2023 (Terry)
Camp 19, ice cap
66° 24.819'N 44° 50.884'W @ 7,772 feet
11.7 miles from camp 18
Total of 167.7 miles
DYE-2 40 miles away
Hill 660 - 150 miles away

WINDY CAMP

What a challenging day!

Woke up to snowfall on the tent with light winds and cold at -5°F.

Skiing started at 0545 with hoarfrost on everything, even on the front of our ski poles. Aaron led the first shift. Very difficult navigation and total overcast. I could see the horizon, but there were no snow features or targets. He's able to keep us moving better.

He started the 2nd shift because of difficult navigation. He continued for a while, but then the light changed and I did the last part of the 2nd shift and 1st part of the 3rd which Aaron finished.

4th shift - Blue sky and warming. Aaron took some layers off and I switched to a lighter balaclava and led. There was a halo around the sun—is this the sign of impending weather?

5th shift - Aaron led. Breeze freshening & cold again.

6th shift - I led. Wind continued to build & Aaron called it so we could build camp before things got really bad. We skied the whole shift but skipped the bonus round.

We built a stout wind wall. Set up the tent. The inside of my vestibule was surprisingly calm. As I'm melting snow and cooking dinner, I wonder what the weather will do. Aaron got a forecast off his GPS—High winds tomorrow. We'll have our first weather day. I had lots of "ear worms" today for the second time this trip. Gross, huh?

Happy with mileages. 5 days in a row of double digits. If we have some endurance, we can make it! Aaron, "Do the shift at the end of the day seem longer because we're traveling further?"

Me, "No. They seem longer because we're tired!"

Day 19 (Aaron)
Wednesday, May 10, 2023

We woke up to a calm, foggy 100% whiteout. We started skiing at 545 a.m. Having no wind makes quite a bit of difference. I only woke up twice to relieve my bladder, then woke at 2:40 a.m. and just prayed for strength, guidance, and safety.

Terry said when I laid down last night, I was asleep in three breaths. I'm sure that's true after two bad nights of sleep in a row.

We covered 11.7 miles. We didn't get our bonus shift in due to high winds, lifting snow two feet off the ground, meaning the wind hit 40 knots.

The first two shifts were in a total whiteout, slowing us down. We are still doing well. It felt like a lot of downhill. A 200-foot elevation loss was crazy. I felt it and loved it. Even though over that distance it's imperceptible, I can feel the difference and see the mileage change. We're already 23.8 miles from the summit.

Terry wasn't as fast today. He said his feet are really hurting. Hopefully his blisters will heal soon. Maybe I should start taking more lead shifts.

It felt like the day would be calm, with a hot shift 3. But, by shift 4, a strong breeze rose up. And, then I noticed the sun bow. Storm coming.

By the end of shift 6 at 330 p.m., the gusts of wind had built up to 35–40 knots. Snow was starting to blow over the sleds. We stopped 10 minutes early to start working on our wind wall.

This wall was 2m thick and 5 feet tall. We're battle-ready. While shoveling, the snow started blowing in our faces.

With Terry's "toy shovel" (as he called it), some nights he can't dig the ice for fear of breaking his shovel. So instead, I do the chipping and digging while he does the engineering. We figured out that if we pile a mount of snow 2 feet tall, then building with semi-cut blocks or snow chunks, we can build a wall far faster than if we just build a rubble pile.

The GPS forecast said there's supposed to be gale-force winds through tomorrow. Is this the piteraq I've feared? I hope not!

I'm jealous of Terry's dinners. He has tuna, fish, meat packs, way better than my plain-freeze dried. Again, I enjoyed my dumplings.

Thursday, 11 May, 2023 (Terry)
Camp 19, Greenland ice cap
Zero day, storm

Glorious rest! A windstorm can be a blessing.

The wind wall held all night and created a crescent drift around the tent. We still need to go out & clean layers of spindrift that have accumulated to 1.5 feet high between the walls of the tent.

When emptying the pee bottle, I noticed my vestibule had unzipped & got it closed. Aaron had more clothes on, so he crawled by me and shoved snowblocks against the vestibule door to prevent that again.

Winds overnight were ~45 knots, gusting to 70! Legitimate "hunker down" decision. Temps were mild in the tent, not outside exposed.

Woke to continuing roaring winds at 3 a.m. and agreed on waiting & checking every 3 hours. I slept on and off until 0900. The weather forecast shows some moderation in winds by this afternoon, but we decided that moving and rebuilding a wind wall in marginal conditions was not worth it. I'd rather ski a couple of longer days to make it up if we have to.

So, a chance to sleep in, let the feet rest and heal, and allow the muscles to recover a bit. This is just what we needed, and probably at the perfect time before our push the rest of the way. God's blessing in a wind storm.

Breakfast & coffee late (0930), then journaling. I have some mashed potatoes we can share for lunch & top it off with roasted wasabi edamame (instead of just eating bars).

Hopefully naps this afternoon.

1430 - We suited up & went to dig out the tent. My sled is half-buried and the windward vestibule was so covered by the snow drift pushing it in that I almost couldn't get out the door. We dug the windward side of the tent out. Between the windfall & the tent wall, the protection system worked spectacularly! The wind wall looks as tall as we built it. Nature filled it in on both sides, so now it's probably 8 meters (25 feet) thick at its base.

We cleaned up some snow away all around the tent but left enough

Day 20 (Aaron)
Thursday, May 11, 2023

The wind blasted last night. Glad we built a 5-foot tall wall that was 2.5m thick, then added wraparounds and lots of chinking. The wind has been 50–70 knots this morning. Last night, I opened the door and the wind choked me out with snow. It started filling the tent immediately. It was around 90 knots. Those were true Phase 2 conditions where I couldn't see my sled. It was nearly pitch black from the density of the snow.

I had put earplugs in to drown out the sound. But, I found waking up around midnight that my ears are so dirty from ear wax that they completely plugged up. So wanting a Q-tip. The only ones Terry brought are dedicated to eye problems, like things in our eyes.

We've decided to take a zero day with the storm raging outside. We can't leave at least until noon to 1 p.m. for 45-knot winds forecast. Then, after skiing for two shifts, we'd have to build another full wind wall under possibly even worse conditions. Terry suggested that didn't make a lot of sense. I wanted to battle it out, but if we get stuck in worsening winds again, that'd be dangerous.

I'm waiting for body functions to work, then I'll go out and see about the wind wall. Definitely don't want to get caught outside needing to go.

The forecast shows the wind is supposed to be like this until the evening, with 45-knot gusts and 35 knots sustained. We don't want to freeze Terry's fingers. He's already having trouble. We've been losing weight, so that's a possible factor, too.

Terry is the best expedition partner. He's smart, patient, insightful, and strong. A very strong 68-year old.

It's still 40 miles to DYE-2, then 150 miles to PT660. We're still good with 2–3 days in reserve.

We rested all day but I don't feel rested at all. The psychological craze of raging winds just wears me out.

We went out to clear snow once. Now, the wind wall is 8m thick (really, yes, 25 feet thick from the buildup). More importantly, it's still 5 feet tall. The design worked just as we'd hoped for, with the forward

to hopefully prevent buildup between the tent walls.

When we were done, we dove back in. I changed to mid-layers and got comfy for lunch. Aaron made water and we stuffed ourselves with mashed potatoes. 4 servings each.

We are relaxing until the evening stove chores. I appreciate that Aaron is always checking on me. How are your hands doing? How are your feet? He's glad I'm getting the complete Arctic travel experience "inside the ping pong ball" conditions.

It's the Arctic cold and wind, and now the windstorm that pinned us down for the day is the experience.

15 days left to go 150 miles. Can we?

Aaron keeps commenting that he really feels like he's skiing downhill sometimes in the last two ski days. The downhill gradient is only 20 feet per mile. It's imperceptible over this uneven terrain.

It's a mix of wind slab, unconsolidated wind-deposited snow, drifts, and sastrugi. So, I just told him that he was just skiing down a wind slab that he just climbed up on. He looked like a kid whose balloon I'd just deflated. But I'm remembering that he never got to experience the long downhill leg of his Antarctica trip, because he ran out of time & couldn't do the return leg from the pole to the coast.

He's really looking forward to the next days when the gradient should be increasingly downhill.

Aaron this morning, "I need to deflate my mate and get it out of the way."

Me, "You should have gotten the auto-deflating model like mine."

Our tent is such a refuge. Aaron said, "It's a tiny red lifeboat on a huge white ocean of ice."

"Love note sent!" To Diane.

Bed at 1930. Still too windy to move. Praying for the winds to ease by morning.

Realized we didn't pack enough dinners (35). Because we ate dinner on day 0. I'll be hungry!

pit dropping snow to thicken things up.

I used my headband to cover my lips last night. They're literally coming off in bloody chunks. Terrible.

The real wind ended up being sustained 45–50 knots with snow high in the air, with gusts well into 60 knots. I got knocked over several times working on the tent, unburying it. We fought the rising wall but it was a troublesome activity.

The wall of ice flying by last night was scary.

We had Terry's Walmart mashed potatoes for lunch. A real, hot lunch. It was smart to eat this and keep the day food for the future [note: this was more important than we realized at the end].

That little thing of instant mashed potatoes was so simple and filling. It allowed us to save an entire day's worth of food each. [Note: even more important for Terry in the end...]

Terry used the cat hole. I didn't. Boo. I was hoping to stay on the morning scheduled but it didn't happen.

We went to sleep at 730 p.m.

Excavating the tent after an Arctic storm event (piteraq).

Friday, 12 May, 2023 (Terry)
Camp 21, ice cap
66° 27.025'N 45° 17.901'W @ 7,500 feet
12.7 miles from camp 19 (storm camp 20)
168.7 miles total
28 miles to DYE-2 @ 276°
138 to Hill 660

Winds seemed to ease at 2200 last night. Awoke to normal light to moderate winds, cold temperatures at -15°F. Late start at 0700. We had to dig the sleds out of the ice, dig out the tent, dig out the stake points, and dig out our ski poles which were buried in the deep drift that formed behind our wind wall.

Wind wall worked very well—it caused the drift to build in front & behind it and directed drifts alongside the tent. Unfortunately, the drift on Aaron's side piled up 2 feet high & thick on the tent wall. Got all the heavy work done & skiing by 0700.

1st shift - Aaron led. Blue sky with fog following us, but easy navigation. My hands stayed frozen the whole shift despite Aaron's Arctic mittens. At one point, I skied up beside him (my shadow startled him) to ask if he could ski faster because I was desperate to get warmer. He said he wasn't feeling it but I think he went faster.

2nd shift - I led and was motivated to ski fast, warming up my hands. Aaron was impressed with the pace, but I was just cold and fresh.

3rd shift - Aaron led. Now he's going out strong. I think he wants mileage. Saw a little songbird on the snow pecking for something to eat. It was probably blown in by the wind storm and lost.

4th shift - I led. Feeling fatigued now but sore feet and blisters much better.

5th shift - Aaron led very strong. I couldn't match his pace.

All day it stayed cool enough to not need clothing adjustments other than venting. It was a nice change.

Surface all day was the same—slick hardback wind slabs alternating

Day 22 (Aaron)
Friday, May 12, 2023

We woke up to a breezy morning, maybe 20-knot winds. After the storm day, this felt perfectly sane.

The tent was buried under 4 feet of compacted spindrift snow. It was rock solid, pushed up against the tent wall. No wonder we couldn't push it back. The good part is our wall held and created a Sastrugi over 150 feet long. That was crazy.

We took an hour to unbury the tent, skis, pulks, and poles. The snow was loose at all like at home in the winter. I could stand on the drift of snow around the tent and on the wall. Our tent completely changed the landscape.

Terry said that the rest did his feet wonders. It showed when he led throughout the day. His speed increases were remarkable. It's like he's a new man on the freshly scoured surface.

He said every day since his blisters set in that starting out was like walking on broken glass. The sides and small vestibule were buried under 4 feet of hard-packed snow. Terry did an excellent job of excavating the ski poles, preventing damage.

I was wasted all day during the first shift. I should have eaten some chocolate to start since we spent an hour excavating.

We saw a Black Phoebe out on the ice. He then visited us at night again. Poor guy must've blown in on the storm. He's a bird visitor like the ptarmigan on the east side of the trip. Hope he makes it!

12.7 miles and a new record! It was a hard surface with lots of small sastrugi. The weather was cool to cold all day.

We got to bed at 7:50 p.m.

I wore my headband around my lips last night. I felt less pain and fewer chunks coming off my lips last the last 2 weeks. It was like the raw pain of rubbing habanero chilies on my lips nonstop. Even drinking water burns them. I'm trying it tonight—wearing the headband around my nose and upper lip. I wear my balaclava pulled over my lower lip during the day for moisture and protection.

with low sastrugi. Good conditions to pull sleds with much effort, but still can't establish much rhythm. I was worried the storm would leave drifts & unconsolidated wind deposit snow for us to slog through, but there was none of that. Aaron said up here, it's the wind that consolidates the snow, but in the lower 48, it's the sun

6th shift - I told Aaron I couldn't match his pace in the 5th session, so he offered to split it up to keep us moving. I did 30 minutes, then him, then I did 15, then he did the bonus round.

Very happy with today's mileage—a new high mark. It was the result of good effort, great surface, good navigations, and conditions that kept us going in a straight line better.

We made camp efficiently so we could get to be earlier after chores. Very tired again. 2000 bedtime.

When the sunset, I could feel the temperature in the tent plummet by the second!

Terry's buried sled at sunset.

Arctic sun dogs.

Aaron all geared up and still smiling after a long day.

Saturday, May 13, 2023 (Terry)
Camp 22, ice cap
66° 26.532'N 45° 41.944'W @ 7,300 feet
11.1 miles from camp 21
Total 179.8 miles
Distance to DYE-2: 17 miles @ 281°
Distance to Hill 660: 128 miles

Happy with today's distance given the poor conditions, snow, and surface conditions. Awoke to light snow & wind, and cold temps. About -10°F.

Aaron took shift 1 - whiteout conditions but led us strong!

I took shift 2. At first, a few navigational targets were visible, but the clouds made them fade in and out. Challenging.

Aaron led shift 3. It was a strong lead & I had trouble keeping up at times. The surface becomes that mix of wind slab, sastrugi, and unconsolidated wind deposits snow. Snow flurries off & on. The wind shifted into our faces from the less. Much less comfortable.

Shift 4 - I lead. There were minimal to no visual targets to navigate by, then total whiteout. I used the texture of the snow at my feet to keep a straight line. Aaron said I earned my navigation while skiing in a whiteout certificate.

Shift 5 - Visibility cleared & Aaron led strong. He was trying to pull me along but I couldn't stay up with him. He took a heavy food bag out of my sled to try to equalize.

Shift 6 - Visibility to whiteout again. Aaron led to strong!

With the wind shifts today, we're not sure where to build the wind wall. It was snowing lightly off & on. The GPS forecast was no help, so we built a second wall off Aaron's vestibule (facing south). I had to boot up again to help Aaron with it. Glad we have a tent that can take a beating.

At bedtime, the winds were calm and there was snowfall. I'm more optimistic we can make it, but Aaron is intent on pushing for 11-mile days & no more storm days. We'll see.

In bed by 2000. I'm comfy in the bag in the tent.

Day 23 (Aaron)
Saturday, May 13, 2023

Today was mentally rough! It snowed all day, adding to the sled drag. Plus, it was a partial to full whiteout all day. Terry did an excellent job of leading into the partial whiteouts. He kept on course, just slower than normal. He's never done the whiteouts + snow + wind battle before this, so it's a real kicker. Kudos to him for braving it out. The whiteout for me was a standard stumble fest. Nothing new. Thankfully the sastrugi were only one to two feet tall.

We hit 11.1 miles today. Woo hoo! It was way short of the 12.7 miles we wanted but with one to four feet of fresh snow, headwinds, and whiteout, we'll take it. We're still above the critical 11-mile-per-day mark.

Terry really slowed down and lost energy. I took on of his partial food bags. I found my ski skins had snow globs. I'm wondering if his skis did, too? I'll fix it tomorrow. It's only 17 miles to DYE-2 and 128 miles to Hill 660. We are 11.5 days away with good sailing weather.

Team of 13 skiers eastbound.

Sunday, 14 May, 2023 (Mother's Day) (Terry)
Camp 23, Ice cap
66° 27.623'N 46° 04.839'W @ 7,130 feet
Distance from camp 22: 10.6 miles
Total distance: 190.4 miles
Distance to DYE-2: 6.6 miles @ 289°
Distance to Hill 660: 118 miles

It was a quiet night with not much wind. A few inches of snow fell gently.

It was very cold, with good visibility when we started skiing at 0550. Aaron estimates -20°F. Luckily there was little wind.

He led shift 1. I had to stop to reconfigure my glove system. I tried a new setup: Thin liners + fleece gloves + Aaron's Arctic Mitts. The setup was too tight & my fingers were in trouble. So, we stopped & I peeled off the liners after windmilling my arms to warm up my fingers. It was much better but my hands were still cold.

It was tough sled-pulling. There was lots of friction with the very cold unconsolidated snow.

Shift 2: I led. It was slow slogging with 1–3" of unconsolidated snow everywhere.

Shift 3: Aaron led. Similar conditions.

Shift 4: I led. Snow flurries & very reduced visibility. There were very few snow lumps to navigate with. I did my best. A C-130 flew low overhead, low enough to see us.

Shift 5 - Aaron led very strong. I had to work to stay up with him. He strengthens and I weaken as the day goes on. Snow flurries continue. The wind freshened and turned into our faces. It was not comfortable.

Shift 6 - I led. Very tired. It was almost a whiteout, so it was tough navigation and really tough going.

Bonus shift - Aaron led. The temperature dropped out with wind in our faces. I was glad to stop and build camp.

I worked on settling into sleep. We need to keep up the pace to make

Day 24 (Aaron)
Sunday, May 14, 2023

It's a beautiful, windless, and cold morning with a lot of snow accumulation to greet us this morning.

Happy Mother's Day, Mom!

We started skiing by 5:50 a.m. with fingers on fire. Terry tried liners in his fleece gloves inside the Altimitts. It was too much pressure and froze his fingers. No damage, though. His fleece gloves aren't like liners, they're actually real gloves. They're too much for the setup. We stopped to get him revived. My fingers were on fire!

It was a nice morning but the ultra-cold snow was like sand. It was brutally slow for 3 sessions. I got warm-ish from exertion, so I had to shed the fleece. I almost shed my parka but glad I didn't. By the 5th session, the threat of overheating was gone. Clouds came in, making it COLD again.

There was a mild headwind to make it more challenging with semi-whiteout conditions. It's tough but manageable.

Terry is struggling with the pace—he said it's a bit fast for him. He said he's running at 80% when he leads which for him is about the max before overload. I'm much faster but I need breaks for overheating.

We hope the bigger downhill starts soon. At least we'll have more oxygen!

We skied 10.6 miles. It's 6.6 miles to DYE-2, 118 miles to Hill 660, about 11 days! That puts us arriving on May 26. There's no more room for storm days, as our pickup is May 27. We're cutting it uncomfortably close.

It's nice in the tent. There are moderate breezes of 20 MPH predicted for the next two days. They're a bit rough but livable.

We hope to find DYE-2 tomorrow. There was a C-130 (Danish?) looping around. It's probably practicing ice landings at DYE-2. Cool. At least we're close!

Hoping for no more delays. Terry's elevation indicates 7,130 feet!

My final lip fix is putting my headband around my mouth at night. It did cause a few breathing panics but it wasn't too bad.

it. We were overall happy with today's mileage, but it doesn't take the pressure off.

We should be able to see DYE-2 tomorrow at midday or so. We're hoping for good visibility so we can find it. Went to bed at 1930.

I need to talk about food. I'm much leaner than we started. I'm curious how much weight I'll shed.

I felt much better about taking the protective tapes off my face tomorrow.

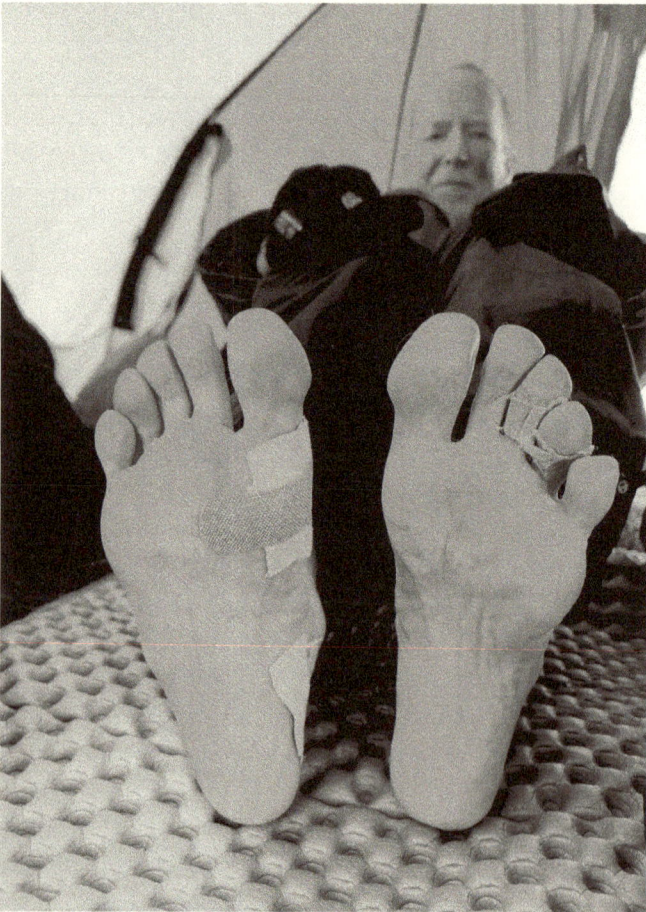

Terry's injured feet.

DYE-2 on the horizon 7 miles (11 km) away.

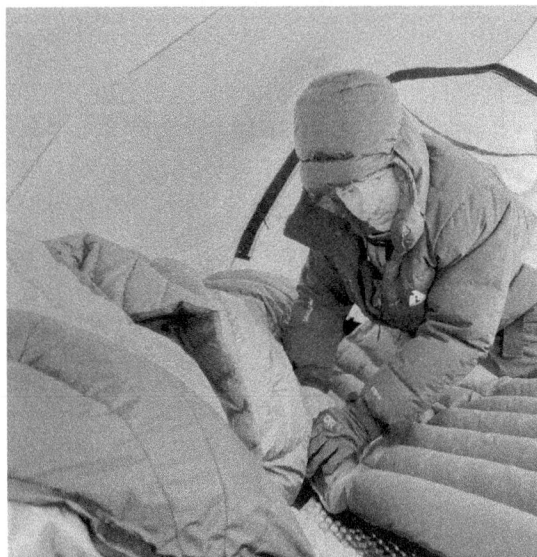

Aaron preparing his bed.

Monday, 15 May, 2023 (Terry)
Camp 24, ice cap
66° 30.721'N 46° 25.286'W @ 6,770 feet
10.1 miles from camp 23
Total mileage: 200.5 miles
DYE-2 reached today
108 miles to Hill 660

It was windy overnight. We woke to a very cold morning with "Sun Dogs" visible in the clear morning sky. It was about -10°F with moderate winds when we started skiing this morning. We both had very cold hands. We had to stop and warm up.

The wind helped with ski and sled dragging conditions. There was very little unconsolidated snow, but there were some wind slabs and sastrugi.

We were able to see DYE-2 on the horizon from camp! Aaron had me check our bearing to make sure it wasn't a polar bear.

We started skiing at 0550. Aaron did the first shift. By the end of the shift, DYE-2 had disappeared below the horizon. The terrain undulates here.

I did the 2nd shift. We could not see DYE-2 at all on the shift.

Aaron did the 3rd shift. It was a faster pace. We spotted DYE-2 on the horizon again. Both of us are having trouble getting consistent compass bearings, so we were off course by about 13°. We checked Aaron's GPS and we saw DYE-2 a few minutes later.

I did the 4th hit. We could see military men working at their camp near the end of a runway, running around on their snowmobiles.

We skied across the runway & on to DYE-2. The wind was strengthening. We skied to the lee side of the building and followed other people's tracks inside. We went up into the radar dome, ate a snack, went outside the hatch, and walked on the balcony. The facility is deceptively huge!

I decided to go back out of the facility and get my headlamp to explore the lower levels. There were frozen cases of food stacked up inside. Many dorm rooms made up the mid-levels, some filled with ice and

Day 25 (Aaron)
Monday, May 15, 2023

It was COLD! and windy. Kinda painful. We saw DYE-2 as we skied our first session. By the 2nd session, we lost it and wandered up to 30° off course. The compasses are working horribly in this cold weather. The errors on the new Suunto MC-3G compass are horrible. Sometimes the needle sticks up to 45° off course. The new design doesn't have a gimbal, just a needle in a hovering cup. Junk for $80.

We saw DYE-2 again and reached it by mid-4th session. It's huge!

Actual DYE-2 location:

N 66.493939°, W 46.321180°

This was 0.5 miles from other reported locations online, including Wikipedia, the bastion of accuracy. Haha.

I found a tear in my parka pocket. :(

I took some cold damage on my lower right back where my exposed skin was weeks ago. I stopped and stuffed my fleece jacket in better. It felt like razor blades slicing my skin.

Once we spotted DYE-2, it took 1.5 sessions to reach it. It's huge and surrounded crevasses and snow caves. It's super cool.

Terry got his headlamp and we explored the dark insides of the monolithic building. We couldn't reach the lowest level at the power plant. We explored the radar dome, electronics room, management rooms, worker dorms, and infirmary. One team marked on the wall they were trapped at DYE-2 for 5 days with 160 KPH (100 MPH) winds.

The facility reminded me of my engineering days at Cubic. I now look fondly back at those days.

The whole building has a slight tilt to it. Kinda disturbing. Make sure to bring a headlamp here. Watch for open panels—I almost slashed my head open hitting a panel Thank goodness for my hat. There's a huge open elevator shaft. Massive fall risk. The stairs are ICY! Terry slipped and fell on some ice. No injury, thank goodness. Loved it!

We skied one more session plus a bonus and got 3 miles!

The big elevation loss, -300 feet, was almost like downhill skiing. We saw 3–4 teams of guided groups. Maybe American and Danish based on the flags?

snow. The facility was abandoned in 1988.

Aaron enjoyed looking at the electronic systems. We were blocked from the lowest levels by ice & snow. The stairways were very icy. I slipped & fell back and hit my head. No damage done.

After touring around, we skied on to this camp and stopped at our normal time. We're very happy with the mileage considering. Skiing from DYE-2 to this camp was fun, as there were fast conditions. But, there was a lot of sastrugi to navigate. Wind continued to strengthen and snow started falling after we got the tent up. We expect winds and snow through tomorrow. We hope to keep up the 11 miles per day average to make it comfortably.

We saw another group of 13 skiers pulling their pulks toward DYE-2 as we skied to camp. So many people!

Aaron is doing some sewing repairs on his parka. I'm ready to sleep!

My favorite dinner tonight—pesto pasta, salmon, olive oil, and Parmesan cheese. It was very good!

I might have miscalculated on the snacks and dinners. The strategy is to keep eating well on ski days. I can go without if needed once we cross the finish line.

Off to bed at 1930. I didn't sleep well last night. The holes in the snow under the tent caused me to slide off my mats and get cold.

Aaron said I fell asleep faster than he could have knocked me out!

Terry (right) and Aaron at DYE-2 station on the Greenland ice cap.

There was a big contingent of military doing flight operations at a graded ice runway. It looked to be about 2 miles long!

I spent the evening sewing up the tear in my parka pocket, using the sewing kit my Mom made for me in Antarctica. Thanks Mom! This should hold up for another 10 days of use.

Terry falls asleep in the noise of the wind storm and bright sunlight in 30 seconds. I'm jealous. I'm too wound up.

We got to sleep at 845 p.m. Praying for better, non-whiteout conditions and weather.

We saw a full set of sun bow and Arctic sun dogs. It was beautiful, though probably indicates poor weather.

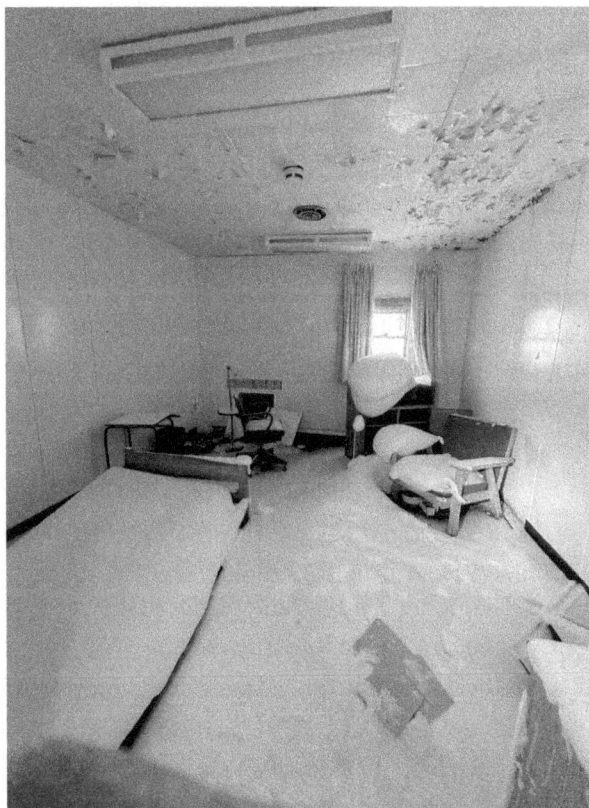

Abandoned DYE-2 station dorm room filled with snow.

Tuesday, 16 May, 2023 (Terry)
Camp 25, ice cap
66° 35.852'N, 46° 47.883'W @ 6,510 feet
12 miles from camp 24
Total of 212.5 miles
96 miles to Hill 660 at a bearing of 294°.

We crossed the Arctic Circle today!

Woke up to moderate windy conditions, clear skies,, and good visibility. We set out skiing at 0600. Winds strengthened and were intimidating with the flat light. There were very few targets to ski ward, so Aaron led. Wind at least 25 knots with temperature around 0°F.

It was great pulk towing conditions—a nice slick surface with the wind at our backs. It felt like we're covering ground easily. It was mostly wind slab and sastrugi.

My hands were very cold. It was very hard to manage in the wind. Aaron felt strong & confident, so he kept leading. I was intimidated by the worsening winds

We passed a large camp heading east during shift 2. It looks like they took a storm day. That's a reasonable plan since the wind would be in their faces.

By shift 3, the wind increased to 40 knots (45 MPH) with gusts to 50 knots. The blowing snow obscured the horizon. It was a tough lead in flat light. All of our breaks were as short as we could manage. My hands are still freezing unless I stop and windmill my arms.

During shift 4, Aaron helped me add pogies to my fleece gloves and mittens. It helped but my hands were still cold.

Aaron kept leading strong despite exhausting responsibilities.

Shift 5 - Horizontal snow with these high winds. But, last least they were at our backs. There were no targets to ski toward with the flat light. I had fun being out skiing and such marginal conditions. I'm confident in Aaron's judgment & experience.

Shift 6 - We slowed down, as Aaron is pretty exhausted with the

Day 26 (Aaron)
Tuesday, May 16, 2023

What a nice morning start. The ground winds were at 20 MPH. We did fine with our breaking camp and were skiing by 6:05 a.m. After shift one, things got spicy. The whole day the wind blew up to 40 MPH with gusts past 50 MPH. It reminded me of Antarctica. I expected that this wind was out of the SSE. If this was in our faces, we'd be in pain.

We passed a guided group camped out. They're smart to stop since they're going uphill and would be in a brutal headwind.

We slugged it out. Terry had to stop and put on pogies with my help to prevent the miserable freeze-thaw cycle he struggles with.

I wore my heavy long underwear today. This was the first day in weeks that my feet weren't cold at all despite the conditions! Using Mom's custom-insulated gaiters and triple socks saved my toes for sure.

I led the whole day. I'm used to this, and I enjoyed the speed. Terry said it cut his stress level down to have me lead so he could enjoy the skiing. We hit 12 miles on what felt like a perpetual downhill. No complaints!

Shift 5, 6, and the bonus shift were a total whiteout on top of the strong wind. Haha! We're getting the full boat experience for sure.

We built a great wind wall, setting up camp starting at 330 p.m., in bed by 730 p.m. It usually takes 40 minutes to build a 5-foot-tall snow wall.

Terry had a great time today. I'm sure glad he's enjoying surviving in these dangerous conditions without injury. I'm happy to lead! The weather from the GPS predicts light to moderate winds for the next 2 days. Woo hoo!

whiteout conditions.

Bonus 30 minutes - The wind moderated & the snowfall stopped in time for us to build camp. (I prayed for this all day).

We built a good wind wall, then crawled into the tent exhausted. The sun came out and warmed the tent.

Winds are now light as we go to bed at 2000.

I'm happy with such good mileage on a challenging day. It's a blessing that the winds were at our backs.

Aaron is great about checking in with me frequently. He just wants to make sure we both go home uninjured.

Hopefully better conditions ahead. We'd like to get there on the 25th, so 9 more days of skiing.

Terry inside the massive DYE-2 radar dome.

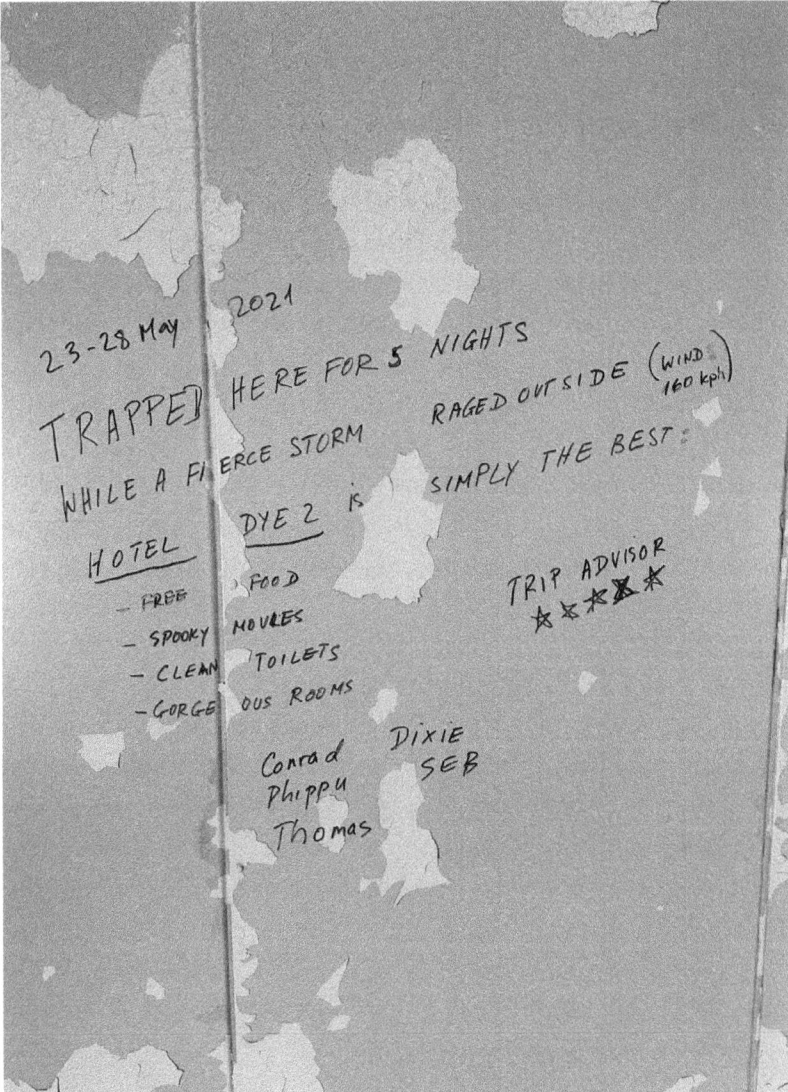

Humor left on a wall by a team trapped at DYE-2 in 2021.

Wednesday, 17 May, 2023 (Terry)
Camp 26, ice cap
66° 39.506'N, 47° 11.074'W @ 6,150 feet
11.4 miles from camp 25
Total 223.9 miles
84.7 miles to Hill 660 @ heading of 295°

We're pleased with today's mileage. We're both exhausted.

It was a quiet night. I woke to little wind, with cold at 0°F. We started out skiing at 0545. Aaron decided to make that a bonus ski time. It was very flat light, so we were unable to see targets to ski toward. There was nothing to ski toward during the whole first shift. It was slow going and Aaron looked tired. He also took the 2nd shift because of navigation difficulty in a whiteout. He checked his watch several times in the long session. His and shoulders slumped when he realized it wasn't over.

3rd shift - I led it. There was more light and I was able to spot targets.

4th shift - Aaron. Strong pace. I had to work to keep up. Still cold hands at times.

(I used fleece gloves, mittens, and pogies during the first two shifts. My hands are cold but not as critical as yesterday).

5th shift - Me. I did okay but I was exhausted at the end. The sliding surface was good but it felt like we were climbing. We got out of the big sastrugi and the surface smoothed over the shift.

6th shift - We split it in anticipation of Aaron doing the bonus round, but he called the day at 1445. We're both exhausted and need some extra sleep.

The afternoon turned sunny and warm, with a light breeze. The tent is too hot to sleep in.

My weight is melting off of me. I have very little abdominal fat anymore and my quads look skinny. I do have some food insecurity. I had to raid the last week's food bag for more daytime food. I also was a bit short in dinner.

My plan was to keep feeding the best until we cross the finish line

Day 27 (Aaron)
Wednesday, May 17, 2023

Decent sleep, though not enough after the wind grinder yesterday. We had a standard morning and were skiing by 5:45 a.m.

We tried a 90-minute session while skiing in a whiteout. That was a mistake! I was crushed by the end. No more 90-minute skis, especially in whiteout conditions for 2 sessions.

Terry took the 3rd session in vague target conditions. He did great and held his speed.

Terry took back the first aid kit, dropping my sled weight by another seven pounds. Yeah!

It was a pleasant day. Nice clouds, a decent cooking breeze. Eventually, we hit an uphill where I overheated. I couldn't figure out why I was stumbling. Then, I realized I wasn't cold enough!

We were both dead at the end of the sixth shift and skipped the bonus. We still got 11.4 miles! We made an elevation of 6,250 feet.

It's really hot in the tent this evening. Whew! But, it is nice though. We have 84 miles to go and 8 days to do it if it all holds well.

The GPS showed a livable forecast, so we're excited.

Sleeping with full gear to combat the cold.

(hopefully early). Then, I can eat the other backup food during the day, like the mashed potatoes, and then divide up the last dinners. We'll do this until our pickup day. I have to keep myself going with food and rest.

Don't know if I've ever felt more physically exhausted. I have to keep moving!

I miss Diane terribly. I just want to sit with her and listen to her talk.

I replaced the diaphragm for the air mat valve. There's nothing to lose. It deflated last night in 20 minutes.

The daily snow wall construction project.

Taking a moment to enjoy the view while Terry prepares his solar panels.

The vastness of the Greenland Arctic ice sheet.

Thursday, May 18, 2023 (Terry)
Camp 27, Ice cap
66° 45.184'N 47° 32.579'W @ 5,660 feet
11.8 miles from camp 26
Total distance 235.7 miles
73 miles to Hill 660 @ 293°

We adjusted our compass declination to 26°W. Really beautiful ski day! I enjoyed myself. It good a good call by Aaron yesterday to call the day early and get some extra rest. We woke to light winds, overcast but good light for navigation. The temperature was more mild, about +10°F. We're dropping elevation daily now, so maybe the bitter cold of the plateau is behind us. We started skiing at 0545.

We traded off ski leads all day. We were happy with our mileage. I didn't push it, as Aaron says, we're too far out for heroic pushes. We need a sustainable pace. It stayed cool enough for nice ski conditions and sled pulling for me in the 4th shift. We saw several ski and pulk tracks nearly parallel to us midday.

In the 5th shift, the sun came out and the wind died, so Aaron needed to stop a few times for clothing sheds.

6th shift - it was warm enough to soften the snow. I was down to a light shirt, light balaclava, boonie hat, and liner gloves.

Bonus shift - Aaron led slowly so he wouldn't overheat and called an end 10 minutes early to set up camp.

Now that we've settled into the tent, the winds are picking up. It's supposed to be windy enough, borderline, that it might pin us down for the next two days. The forecast calls for sustained 35 MPH with gusts to 45 MPH. This was actually a little less than we skied in on the windy day, so we're planning to go. We'll reassess in the A.M.

Prevailing winds out of the southeast. It'll be at our backs and much more tolerable.

Got to bed at 1900. I started eating into the last food sack. The end is in sight. No luck on the sleeping pad. It quickly deflates.

Day 28 (Aaron)
Thursday, May 18, 2023

What a nice chilly morning! Though it was overcast, there was enough light coming through the cloud cover to prevent a full white-out for the first 2 shifts. What a welcome change!

The surface was nice and mostly sastrugi-free all day. By shift 5, the temperature rose as the wind dropped, slowing us down a bit.

We covered 11.8 miles, leaving 73 miles to the finish line. We're still projected to be done on May 25, 7 days away. Going to be very tight on food.

Terry did a great job on his leads. I was only skiing right behind him for the last 15 minutes of his shift. In session 6, I had to drop all of my jackets. It took me a full 18 minutes to catch up with him. He's doing great!

I was roasting hot in the last sessions, so we quit with 10 minutes left in the bonus session.

At 7 p.m., it's already windy. It's supposed to be 35 MPH winds with 50 MPH gusts through tomorrow morning. It'll be rough, similar to our killer day a few days ago.

We lost 500 feet to 5,761 feet. Woo hoo! 7 days to go, barring a serious storm.

I miss everyone back home. Mom's custom-insulated gaiters saved my toes from frostbite today. Brr! The wool kartankers aren't holding up well. Plus, they just don't insulate like Terry's Intuition liners.

We got to sleep at 6:50 p.m.

An ocean of sastrugi to ski across.

Friday, 19 May, 2023 (Terry)
Camp 28, ice cap
66° 48.412'N 47° 45.104'W @ 5,495 feet
6.8 miles from camp 27
Total distance 242.5 miles
66.4 miles to Hill 660, new heading 292°

Roaring wind and blowing snow all night. It was tough for either of us to sleep. My vestibule door blew open twice. Aaron had the solution—open the little vestibule window and shove ice chunks outside onto the door. It wasn't easy. Meanwhile, I hid from the spindrift snow in my sleeping bag.

He checked the weather at 3 a.m. and we decided to wait an additional 3 hours to let the winds die down from 50+ MPH.

We didn't have much trouble digging out the tent and got started at 0900.

Aaron took the first shift with flat light and no visible navigation targets. It was about +10°F.

The light was better on the 2nd shift, so I was able to lead okay.

3rd shift things started to deteriorate again with flat light, making navigation difficult. The wind shifted from southeast to southwest, so it was it was in our faces. Winds started picking up, driving the snow horizontally.

We talked about today's schedule. Aaron wanted to do the full 6.5 shifts. However, with our late start, I argued that we'd only get 4 hours of sleep instead of the usual 7. We decided on doing 5 shifts.

I tried to start shift 4, but with the high wind and snow in our faces, I couldn't keep my face from freezing. The only way I avoided the face freeze was to look down and to the right to keep the fur ruff over my face.

The conditions continued to deteriorate with wind, snow, and little visibility as Aaron led. Winds built to 35 MPH with gusts up to 50 MPH.

I called a conference and said we needed to stop and make shelter. Aaron argued that we HAVE TO do our 6.5 shifts if we're going to make it. I argued that we need to have a climber's attitude—take what the day

Day 29 (Aaron)
Friday, May 19, 2023

It was more lack of sleep. Last night, the wind whipped up to a real storm at 50+ MPH. Screaming.

The snow wall had decent-sized holes in it. The snow berm didn't have time to self-build, as the wind rose too quickly.

Terry's door seal failed. The door unzipped. He closed it. But then it unzipped again. I woke up hearing a rattle. He told me it had opened. I looked. The snow on his vestibule was gone and nothing was protecting the door.

Spent 15 minutes digging a pit and putting up a fast wall of snow to secure the door. I shoveled snow blocks through the window to stabilize the vestibule.

That was a rough activity to take care of at midnight. We were lulled into a false sense of security with the windless hot afternoon. The forecast said these winds were 35–40 MPH. No way. They're rushing by at 50–60 MPH to tear open the door like that.

We "slept" until 6 a.m. The wind was still 50 MPH at 7 a.m. Ouch.

We rolled out at 9 a.m. with hopes of easing conditions.

The first shift was fully blind. Terry didn't lead the 2nd shift due to whiteout with sticky snow. I even got too hot in these freezing conditions.

Terry is really moving fast now. In the 3rd shift, we were blind with building snow. By the 4th shift, it was really bad. Terry tried to lead but he was fully blind. I took over. I stumbled on for 75 minutes. Terry suggested we call it, as the conditions had turned into a full storm. We built a massive wall to get better sleep. I'm way fatigued.

We covered 6.8 miles. Crosswinds were 40 MPH. They kept knocking me over. Looks to still be rough tomorrow. We're praying for a window of good weather to cover another 11-mile day.

The GPS weather suggested winds above 30 MPH well past noon. That's going to make a tough farewell tour from Greenland.

Terry's sled was covered in water, even in this crazy storm. That's how strong the sun is. But, when I removed my fleece jacket, the wind burned my left arm. It was intense and similar to South Pole conditions.

gives and be satisfied.

Aaron relented and we made camp in worsening conditions. We built a stout wind wall and crawled in.

As we crawled into bed, the wind was still blowing and it was a white-out. It's supposed to be bad through the night and into the morning.

If we can be productive for the next 6 days doing 11 miles per day, we'll get there on the 25th. We need rest, food, and better conditions to make it.

It was tough to build a wall in whiteout conditions. We couldn't see it! It felt like we built the "Great Wall of China."

Partial construction of the "Great Wall of China" wind wall.

We need more sleep and better conditions. I love the wildness of the terrain and weather, we just are short on time.

We were glad for the huge snow wall, so we weren't worried about the wind. It made the tent much calmer.

Arctic sunrise.

Saturday, 20 May, 2023 (Terry)
Camp 29, ice cap
66° 53.115'N 48° 07.535'W @ 5,036 feet
11.6 miles from camp 28
Total 254.1 miles
55.2 miles to Hill 660 @ 290°

It was a wild night of wind that calmed by the time we got out mercifully. It was below 0°F and stayed cold like that all day.

Aaron was excited to see a sun pillar and sun dog during the rising sun when we went out. We had to dig out, but it was easier than the last windstorm. My sled was completely buried and invisible next to the vestibule door. In spite of all that, we got skiing at 0630.

Even though I armored up in liners, mittens, and pogies, it wasn't enough. At the end of the first break, I had to swap the liners for thin fleece gloves to add warmth. This was the first day I had to wear that combo all day. Aaron took the first shift as usual so he could lead in the flat light and difficult navigation conditions. The surface was good with hard wind slab and limited Sastrugi or unconsolidated snow.

2nd shift I took - there was better light and more visible navigational targets. It started snowing and the loose snow started piling up, making sled towing much more difficult.

3rd shift - Aaron led. Snow and wind increased with a solid whiteout. He still led strong.

4th shift - I tried but my face was freezing and east wind blowing snow in our faces at the left quarter. I turned it over to Aaron so we could make more progress. He ended up leading the rest of the day due to the headwinds.

I could barely keep up with his strong pace. He's in his element when things are cold and difficult. Later...

Now that we're in the tent, the wind has calmed. We're happy with our mileage despite the very tough conditions. I re-assessed my food supply. I should have enough to eat it we make it in 5–6 days and are careful.

Got into bed at 2000 despite the late start. I'm hoping for improved navigation and sled pulling conditions as we head for the finish line!

Day 30 (Aaron)
Saturday, May 20, 2023

What a perfect Arctic sunrise. There was a sun pillar with a left-side sun dog. Plus, the sky was hazy with sub-zero temperatures. Brr! It was so perfectly beautiful, I teared up. It was exactly the sunrise I had dreamt about for over three years to enjoy just one single morning.

It was cold, a whiteout, with 30 MPH south winds. And, the snow was at least 10 inches deep all day. Yet, we made 11.5 miles!!

Terry led the fifth shift, but the sky turned to a full whiteout, finally stopping him. The crosswind is burning his face. He can't fold out his fur ruff like my Alaska Raw Fur parka. Rough!

I enjoyed the lead. Terry's fatiguing out today and is now constantly hungry. He's dipping into tomorrow's food. That's kinda risky!

If the weather holds, we can make dirt in five days. Please hold! The snow drifts were absurdly deep today. I end up with huge globs of snow on the bottom of my skins.

This was a tough day yet it was a joy to ski. Terry's following hard and says he's running at 90% of capacity. He's having trouble even keeping up with me after I've dug out a snow track for him to follow. Hopefully he's still having fun with this?

In theory, we will lose 4,000 feet over the next five days. That's about 800 feet per day.

We hit the sack at 8 p.m.

Traveling from the edge of the Earth.

Sunday, 21 May, 2023 (Terry)
Camp 30, ice cap
66° 55.974'N 48° 27.221'W @ 4,725 feet
9.5 miles from camp 29
Total 263.6 miles
45.9 miles from Hill 660 @ 290°

It was final exam day! The winds calmed during the night. We woke up late at 0320, causing us to start skiing late at 0615. It was flat light with no targets to ski toward. We enjoyed a corn snow surface with snow flurries.

It ended up snowing all day on us. The aftermath was more corn snow and the lightest powder I've ever seen in my life. The wind freshened and was in our faces for session 2. Combined with the whiteout, it was very uncomfortable travel. Maybe -10°F.

By session 3, we had an "in the ping pong ball" experience. Aaron said he hoped the ice cap wouldn't give us a final exam, but she did.

The sun peaked out briefly to show how pretty the new 5" of snow was, then socked in again. Aaron led all day. He's able to ski a straight line in a total whiteout. I either ski in a circle or stop.

Really poor sled pulling conditions all day. There was a lot of friction. Session 5 was particularly arduous and felt like it was uphill.

So no wonder why our mileage suffered today. Aaron was disappointed in our progress. But, he made a heroic effort today. If I'd led, we wouldn't have made as much progress.

We built our wind wall and set up the tent in a continued whiteout. There's no wind as we go to bed. The GPS forecast predicted the wind would come up at night and go all day. At least it was supposed to be from the ESE, so at our backs.

We're getting shot in food supplies. We need to make it in 4 days if we can. Need better snow conditions. Maybe the wind will scour the soft snow away and consolidate the rest?

To bed at 0730. Exhausted, grimy, and dirty.

Day 31 (Aaron)
Sunday, May 21, 2023

I'm amazed how there is little to no ice and snow buildup on Terry's ski skins. I'm fully wondering if he ended up with the pure mohair rather than the nylon blend. By shift 5, I had 6 inches of ice attached to the bottom of my skis. It's rough.

It was cold this morning but I was able to remove my fleece after shift one. There wasn't much wind. Then, during the ski session, the breeze came up and my toes started to freeze. Ouch!

The snow is deep, from 8 to 12 inches. Plus, it was a whiteout most of the day. It sure made for engaging skiing. It kept my mind busy. It was crazy-tough pulling. I had to double-pole every obstacle. I laughed every time I got hung up—what else was there to do?

Plus, it seems that there were rolling hills and large hidden sastrugi. We only lost 300 feet over 9.5 miles. We hoped for 11 miles, but the snow depth just sacked us.

We are still alive, but the short days created a 2-mile deficit. We're facing running out of food on the last day except for my bags of food-forward scraps. We are praying for no more bad weather for 5 days.

Getting hung up was the max load workout all day. I was still good but pushing the limits of what I could drag. Terry is as tough as ever. He's doing a great job.

I had to start looking at my skis for a 15 count, then I was able to keep a much straighter line than looking at the horizon. This is a new trick! What a great discovery.

There were no navigational targets to ski toward, so it was a full whiteout the rest of the day. All day. I loved it. Woo!

I miss everyone back home so much.

In bed by 7:30 p.m.

Monday, May 22, 2033 (Terry)
Camp 31, ice cap
67° 00.377'N 48° 50.669'W @ 4,150 feet
11.8 miles from camp 30
Total mileage 275.4
33 miles to Hill 660 @ 287°

The weather prediction was for high winds this AM and we got them. They started up at 1 a.m. The tent performed great. They were hitting the tent broadside and we barely felt it inside.

Started skiing at 0600. My hands were frozen by the time we dug out the tent and broke camp. Winds were a sustained 25–30 MPH with gusts to 45 MPH. The temperature was -10°F so it was a wicked windchill.

I changed into my fleece gloves, mittens, and pogie combo in the lee side of the wind wall. It was painful to have to go down to bare skin in these conditions. Aaron always helps me with the second pogie. He led for the first two sessions because I was at the edge of freezing my hands and face. Fortunately the wind was out of the ESE, at our backs.

I led the third session. My hands improved and I windmilled (flapped) my arms during the breaks. The wind provided great sled pulling conditions. We did have to navigate around large rounded sastrugi in one area.

Aaron led the fourth session. We both noticed the terrain started rolling as we approached the coast and we were towing uphill.

I led the 5th session. I was very tired towing uphill.

6th session we split.

At 1425, we topped a rolling hill and spotted coastal mountains! This is the first thing we've seen on the plateau for a month. It was great to ski some downhill in the 6th and bonus sessions. It was a taste of the next few days.

It was sunny with calm winds when we made camp. We built a small wind wall and called it good to save energy. We re-assessed our food supplies. We can feed ourselves fully for 3 days, so if it takes longer, we'll be hurting. It's supposed to snow tomorrow. It may slow us down but we need 11-mile days. We went to bed at 1930. I rotated my base layers.

Day 32 (Aaron)
Monday, May 22, 2023

As the Weather inReach GPS (weather genie) predicted, the wind began at midnight and built to 25 to 35 MPH gusts by the time of our departure. We mistakenly built the wall for the evening wind rather than the prevailing sastrugi. The tent was broadsided all night but held up well.

We were up at 3 a.m. as usual. I had to dig out my sled. It was cold! I even used my heavy long underwear, a risk for overheating later in the day. Terry's hands were frozen for two sessions until the wind calmed by the third. He led that one and was fast. He said, "I am cold-motivated!"

I can feel the fatigue of the last few days of foot-deep snow and whiteouts. It was great to have Terry blazing a trail again. It's relaxing to follow him, even in tough conditions.

Yesterday, we heard a bird for the first time. It was above our heads in the clouds. We joked it was squeaking ski bindings. We're still over 40 miles out. Terry spotted land at 2:25 p.m. Coastal mountains to the south. Woo hoo!

There were some steep downhills. I kept getting knocked down by my sled. We saw our first patches of blue ice!

The camp was very nice. It was quiet. We're 34 miles out and tight on food. I have 2 dinners but 4 days of regular day food. Terry has 2 days of regular day food and 4 dinners. Haha!

Looks like we'll make landfall Thursday. In 3 days, if possible. Hopefully there's no wild weather to battle. Terry's GPS said we lost 600 feet today. My GPS shows wild land contours, so we should drop quickly.

I had the beef stew tonight. It only had 420 calories. Totally not satisfying. After 45 minutes of finishing dinner, I was hungry again. The beef dinners don't cut it. I need more calories.

Terry has been hungry for at least two weeks and has eaten through a full day's rations to bolster his low-calorie load. He had a meal plan that ended up with the lightest calories at the end of the trip. Oops!

We got to bed at 7:20 p.m.

Tuesday, 23 May, 2023 (Terry)
Camp 32, ice cap
67° 02.463'N 49° 50.464'W @ 3,485 feet
11.4 miles from camp 31
Total distance 268.8 miles
Distance to Hill 660: 22.6 miles @ 290°

It was a hard day for both of us. Guess the "Final Exams" continues. With this much elevation loss, we expected easier sled pulling, but we only got 45 minutes of that.

The snow was predicted and it came. Temperatures we mild, about +10°F with some cloud cover. The worst part was the winds came from the NW, driving winds into our faces. I couldn't keep my nose from freezing, so I had to stop and dig out my goggles. They worked well with my balaclava.

There was a whiteout all day. The snowfall ranged from gentle flurries to all-out blizzard. Aaron did a heroic job of leading all shifts. It's amazing how he can generally keep moving straight in those conditions.

His technique is to ski 15 steps and review his compass.

We hit large areas where we had to plow through unconsolidated snow and large drifts, including climbing a couple of hills. The effort level was very high.

We also hit interesting areas of exposed blue ice rising up in lumps. Maybe they were pressure ridges?

To keep the goal in range, we did a full 7th session to get in another 1.5 miles. So, we skied from 0545 to 1600.

Aaron helped me out with some chocolate at the start of the 7th shift since my daytime food is too short for that snack. It keeps me going.

With the weather looking settled (the snowstorm is supposed to end at midnight) and winds are supposed to stay light, we skipped the exertion of building a wind wall.

We put up the tent and got busy with our stoves melting snow for water for tomorrow and re-hydrating dinner.

We're hoping for better visibility and a sliding surface for the next

Day 33 (Aaron)
Tuesday, May 23, 2023

It was a relatively warm morning but it snowed ALL night. We woke to a 100% whiteout. I lead all the shifts plus the bonus session. Terry said he was red-lining how fast he could ski following me. He said that there was no way he could lead at this speed.

We were fast and clocked 9.8 miles by the end of shift 6. To underscore, we made it to 11.4 miles by the end of shift 7! We seemed to have climbed a massive hill but still 650 feet over the day. The huge uphill meant we skied down some steep stuff.

We found a bunch of lumpy blue ice that looked ethereal in the full whiteout.

We had driving snow into our faces 100% of the day. Terry switched to goggles which saved his face.

I can't use goggles while I'm pulling at 90% power with the sun out. They just steam up even when I'm shivering. I definitely don't have the best body for this.

Terry started the trip only peeing once a night. Now, he said he's going four to five times a night. Welcome to the club, buddy!

He also frostbit his left cheek today and shows frost injuries on his thumbnail and most fingers. He's riding the absolute edge of frostbite with his hands.

I should have asked him use his mittens and pogies earlier on in the trip. It's caught up with him.

We're both having trouble staying warm [I lost 25 pounds by this point]. I used mittens for all but shift 6 and 7. Brr!

Terry said his gloves aren't warm anymore. They're totally greased out like my gloves. It's going to be cold travel.

It was a rough day all around with a headwind, whiteout, driving snow, and over a foot of loose drifted snow to plow through. I kept counting to 15, correcting my course with my unreliable compass, all while looking at my ski tips for nearly 10 hours straight.

We only had a short reprieve in the blue ice field. That is when I can see them at all.

We have 22.4 miles to go. We must make it by Thursday or we'll be

two days. If so, we should make the finish line by Thursday afternoon.

We hope to call and change our pick up to Friday since we'll be out of food.

Bed at 1940.

Terry stomping soft snow for a more comfortable night on the ice.

out of food.

I gave Terry some of my chocolate to eat. He had nothing left to eat for the bonus session. Ouch! I keep 3 cookies for later instead of eating them earlier, so that's how I keep myself going.

We got to bed by 7 p.m. It's still snowing at 8 p.m. It does create an epic landscape.

(Top) Last campsite on the ice.

(Right) The nightly pile of gear we slept on.

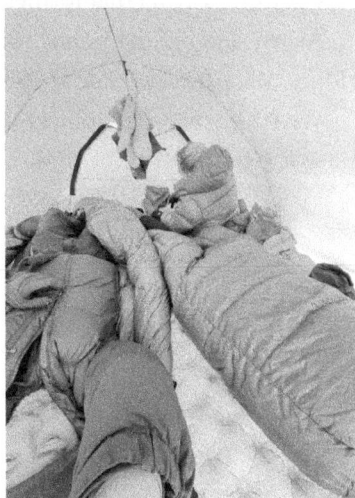

Wednesday, 24 May, 2023 (Terry)
Camp 33, ice cap
67° 06.726'N 49° 38.111'W @ 2,888 feet
11.3 miles from camp 32
Total 298.1 miles
Distance to Hill 660: 11.4 miles @ 284°

Drifts and pressure ridges

We hoped for slick sled pulling and visibility with the wind at our backs. We got the last two.

We alternated leads so Aaron could get some breaks.

We hit a lot of undulating terrain and piles of unconsolidated snow. The drifted snow was up to 1.5 feet deep which really slowed us down. There were some tantalizingly slick spots but most of it was high-effort slogging.

I was able to drop the Pogies by shift 3 so I could ventilate. We both dropped our parkas by shift 5. There was a cool wind blowing but not wasn't strong enough to keep us cool at this effort level.

We did a 7th shift today so we could keep the goal in range tomorrow because there are 45 MPH winds predicted for two days from now. We got into a large area of "disturbed ground." They were large ice pressure ridges with sastrugi that formed big holes to fall into.

Aaron also led the bonus round into camp among the ice pressure ridges. We got to bed late at 2030.

We HAVE to finish tomorrow. It'll probably be a long day but it will be worth it to finish.

Ice pressure ridges over 30 feet (9 m) tall.

Day 34 (Aaron)
Wednesday, May 24, 2023

It snowed several inches last night. Boo. The wind was light which was good since we skipped on building a wind wall. The Garmin in-Reach predicted light winds and was correct. What a time and energy salvation.

The snow was up to a foot deep which made for crazy snow towing. I switched from pushing my skis to lifting them up on every step. I walked with them like snow shoes. The total energy use was less even though I lifted the skis. The ultimate workout slog. I laughed the whole time.

There are no gimmes in Greenland. I think we've maybe had two perfect ski days during the whole trip. Even then, it gets soft in the afternoon. I didn't like it at first, but now I embrace it as a worthy challenge. We hit a massive ice-lump field in the afternoon. There were 9-foot deep holes. It was crazy. There's an open zone of land to the north. Maybe easier travel. Blue ice lumps are the most interesting landscape of the entire trip.

The Garmin weather says that Thursday will be good weather, followed by 35–45 MPH winds with a total whiteout on Friday. So, we have to be out on Thursday no matter what. The landscape looks insane with 50-foot drops. We can't do that blind. It'll be a massive final run!!

Terry did great leads today. He's motivated & hungry. We're nearly out of food. He has one day of food left. I have 2.5 days of food left. He has 3 dinners. I now have ZERO dinners.

We have plenty of fuel for water—whew! Learning not to heat up the water too much from Terry has been a huge fuel saver. Thanks Terry! We did 7 shifts and an additional half-hour bonus shift to get our 11.3 miles. Brutal! We have 11.4 miles to go in huge ice lumps and glacier fall. It's going to be a long day tomorrow.

We got to sleep at 8:45 p.m. Very late for us, but getting the extra miles was worth it.

My lips got ruined again today. I'm literally tasting blood and feeling chunks of my lips tear off. Eating and drinking hurts. I must look like the explorers of the Edwardian Great Age of Polar Exploration.

Thursday, 25 May, 2023 (Terry)
Camp 34 @ Hill 660
69° 09.083'N 50° 02.538'W @ 1,630 feet
11.3 miles from camp 33
Total 309.4 miles

Strategic retreat

What a day! I'm writing this from the morning of May 26 at Hill 660.

There was bright sunshine, the wind was at our backs, and the temperatures were mild at +10°F as we started. It was still cold enough to need Pogies for the first 2 shifts.

We started at 0600. We made a mistake going deeper into this pressure ridge area of the glacier. The terrain became impassible with huge ice bulges and sastrugi that formed pseudo-crevasses that finally stopped us. We made the hard decision to backtrack and head toward clear ground.

It was a long slog to it. We skied until 2 p.m., maybe adding 6–8 miles of travel. Aaron kept wanting to turn our bearing but there was still difficult ground in that direction and we are still 8.5 miles from the finish. We finally got clear and turned our bearing.

Still, the day turned into a constant struggle with route finding. It was like navigating an icefall without the crevasse and collapse dangers.

Impassable huge ice bulges are all around us. Aaron kept finding a way. Sometimes we had to take off our skies and claw our way up an ice hump. We dragged our sleds behind, ultimately skiing all the way to Hill 660 with no crampons needed.

We found the footpath and camped next to it. We had our skis off at 2230. We still had water to prepare and dinner to cook. (Aaron is out of dinners.) I did mashed potatoes and pesto pasta.

I am out of day snacks. Aaron had extra and kept feeding me lots of chocolate. I've never wolfed down that much chocolate in my life!

We got to bed at 0200. It was the most amazing day of skiing and route-finding in my life! What a way to finish!

Day 35 (Aaron)
Thursday, May 25, 2023

We were up at 3 a.m. The sky was perfectly clear with a light breeze. Couldn't have asked for a nicer travel day. We started skiing at 6 a.m. and finished at 1030 p.m.

What an epic! We took the northern route down the glacier. That was the most difficult route finding & travel of my life.

Terrain traps, huge chasms, walls, drop-offs, ridges, and out-of-control sleds. This final day gave me everything I ever wanted and more. Terry had a much better time with his more forgiving bungee rig setup. Mine was punishing as ever, rigged for pure uphill travel.

Terry ran out of food, so I supplied him from my food-forward bag.

We arrived at Hill 660 on the north side. Terry wandered to the south side of the hill and found poles, flags, and the trail. Super cool!

We made it!

When Robert of The Red House said to take the right side down the glacier, we should have asked him to point out the route on a map. Was that looking west or looking east? We learned it was looking east. Oops—The Greenlandic language is relativistic, so we didn't know where the reference point was. Bummer. As we learned, it was the south side of the ice cap edge near Hill 660 that's passable.

I was running at 95% capacity all day leading. Terry wanted me to lead through the day. It was good because I can move faster and I have the height advantage for sighting.

The landscape was surreal and huge. Where the GPS showed tighter contour lines, the landscape was super steep. It was barely controllable with skis and a pull.

It was tough and totally memorable. There were holes and walls 200 feet tall, the smaller ones being 20 to 50 feet tall. Virtually the entire landscape was impassible.

My biggest fear was becoming completely terrain-trapped. We did get trapped initially when we moved 3 miles west from camp to the WNW. We ran into 20 to 30-foot-tall blue ice escarpments we simply couldn't ski past.

As we discovered later in the day, those earlier walls were

Terry surveying the unreal landscape 5 miles (8 km) from the finish.

Dragging a sled through steep, difficult terrain.

modest-sized compared to the ones we encountered closer to the west end of the ice cap. Many grew to 100 to 200 feet tall in the distance.

We were super blessed to get through the northern edge. Amazingly, this part of the ice cap doesn't flow, so there are no true crevasses and cracks so common with other flowing glaciers. This is why expeditions also use this area as an entry or exit.

We skipped our last few breaks after 6 p.m. and pushed through hunger and dehydration to keep ourselves moving. Nearly five straight hours of non-stop skiing, climbing, crawling, sliding, and having the journey of our lives. We arrived at Hill 660 after descended the last icefall and area as steep as a black diamond ski run. The descent down the last part was wildly steep. It would've taken crampons to ascend this area.

Terry's more forgiving tow line setup that had more stretch in it made travel easier for him. He was only knocked off his feet a few times. I was punished with a constant battle. My setup is perfect for uphill. Just enough stretch to take out the shock but nothing more to waste energy. But on downhills this steep, when my sled took off ahead of me, the impact shock knocked me off my feet. Endless stress. It was great for Antarctica and Denali but not the last day of Greenland.

I could spend a week photographing this area with monumental ice slopes. It's just access is so difficult and expensive. It would simply take too long to ascend and descend to photograph during the day. A few weeks later, the frozen water pools would thaw and create uncrossable barriers. It would require crampons and ice axes, causing far slower travel.

Even though I bemoaned the foot-deep snow that fell a few days ago, it was THE EXACT that made the final descent possible.

Terry's idea of moving north into the open region initially worked until we were 6 miles out at 237°. I told him we had to turn into the crazy terrain and go directly to make it. It was already 4 pm. We were out of time.

It turned out to be a good decision. The farther north we went, the tougher the landscape became.

The southern area was more open. In retrospect, it was simply a

The thrill of victory at 2 a.m. after skiing for 16 hours.

far easier landscape to pass after talking with others. Oops. I failed to collect the most important piece of data for the entire trip—the exact details on the beginning and the end. Other tips weren't like this, so I learned.

I was glad to have fully charged my GPS. I ran it from 91% down to 54% during the day. We needed it constantly to correct our bearing given the wild terrain. We simply couldn't travel in a straight line. We had to take quarter-mile diversions around ice mountains and deep valleys.

As we arrived at camp once Terry found where we were supposed to go, we shuffled around and found a wonderfully wind-free location. Just a dozen yards north had 35 MPH winds all night.

Pitching the tent was tough, as the ice had gone through substantial freeze-thaw cycles. And, the snow was really dirty, making finding ice for water difficult.

We made our hot water. Terry generously shared his mashed potatoes and pesto pasta for dinner. I could've eaten my next day's snacks, but he insisted. It was a good trade, as I gave him snacks all day. It balanced out. He achieved zero food on the last ski day. It was scary to be that tight.

Hill 660 wasn't quite the lush paradise we had hoped for.

Friday, 26 May, 2023 (Terry)
Hill 660 near Kangerlussuaq, West Greenland

I tried to sleep in but I woke at 0300 and checked my watch. Slept on until 0700 or so and stirred. Aaron was up and heard voices. There was a guided group of Germans who just finished and are hanging out here.

We had breakfast and then Aaron called Old Camp Lodge. They didn't have room for us tonight, but we can get a ride into town with this German expedition at 1500.

Guess we'll sleep in the tent one more night...

Aaron texted Diane that we'd finished. I'm hoping to text her from town again. I'm longing to hear her voice again.

We lugged our packed pulks over a terminal glacial moraine to the vehicle. It was the toughest quarter mile of my life! The ride to town was beautiful. We saw a pair of reindeer calves alongside the road, several more adult reindeer, a reindeer carcass being fed on by ravens, a few musk ox, and an "Arctic desert" area of sand dunes and a dry riverbed.

It turned out that the lodge did have room for us after all. After unloading and giving us our room key, Adam (the Arctic bus driver) gave us a bag with two long sandwiches in it because he knew we'd be hungry. Nice!

We devoured them in the lodge, then hopped a bus to the airport cantina and ate a huge musk ox sandwich and fries. I also ate Aaron's fries, too, and chased it all with a beer.

Back at the lodge, I did a partial shave and shower for the first time in over a month! I'm ready for bed!

Day 36, May 26, 2023 (Aaron)

No more skiing, we are here!!

Going to bed at 2:30 a.m. meant we were both destroyed.

I shared my last half-dozen shortbread cookies with Terry for breakfast. I had my last cereal, Nido whole powdered milk, and 3 tablespoons of sugar for breakfast.

Around 10 a.m., I thought I started hearing voices. At first I attributed it to being deliriously tired. Then, I realized they were real. I stuck my head out and learned they were a German team. They had skied for over 24 hours, covering 40 km (25 miles) according to them. They were tall, strong, and in their late 20s. They did this to beat the incoming storm and whiteout that was upon us.

They took the smarter southern route to our more adventurous northern route. When I told them which way we went, they were shocked.

"Well, there are many ways to travel out here. That was an interesting way," the lone team woman said.

I made our single satellite phone call to Old Camp for a pickup. They said they had no rooms? How was this possible? It's a huge location. Maybe there was a set of flights canceled due to weather?

We had 2 hours to relax, then we packed and began the brutal process of hauling our pulks over a very rudimentary glacier moraine trail. It was a quarter-mile rock and dirt crawl over a 400-foot tall pass to the road's end from Kangerlussuaq. That was crazy tough to do as the final surprise bonus round. Even the five strong Germans struggled mightily. They had musical instruments with them and were a fun group.

I met Sven, a German father on the bus. He shared his wisdom of the Arctic, pointing out reindeer, musk ox, and how he got her. When he first arrived, he believed every rock was a musk ox. Adam, our driver, took me away from the group. He secretly said we in fact did in fact have a room. Woo hoo!

We were in the ULO lodge house. This is the famous Old Camp expedition lodge, one I had stayed in nearly 16 years before. Sweet. He even brought us ham and pickle sandwiches to be eaten after we'd been dropped off. Super nice. They thought of everything.

Two friends celebrating success after a five-week Arctic expedition.

There were a lot of flight cancellations, so the entire four Old Camp dorm buildings were full.

Later, after eating our spectacular pickle, ham, and cheese sandwiches, we caught a bus to the airport. Some Danish guys invited us to the only other restaurant on the south side of town. We passed so Terry could get his much-anticipated shower.

We did enjoy our musk ox sandwiches. The downside was by the time we were done eating, the bus stopped running. We had to walk back 1.3 miles to Old Camp on the windy and dusty road. Since the lodge was so full, it took 2 hours after we returned before we could take our showers.

Finally, we slept in real beds at 10 p.m. It was so bright, we had to draw the blackout shades. The night was never dark above the Arctic Circle in June. It was always like near-sunset light in the lower 48.

Saying farewell to the ice cap while riding on a massive Arctic bus.

Saturday, 27 May, 2023 (Terry)
Old Camp Lodge, Kangerlussuaq

The place was full overnight. It was travelers stuck by weather delays. After breakfast this morning, we were the only ones left in the building.

We enjoyed a breakfast of bread, cheese, jam, honey, and muesli, with endless coffee and orange juice. We went into town to take care of errands.

I didn't realize what an issue it would be to ship the gun back to Robert at The Red House in Tasilaq. It's Saturday and the post office is closed. We ran down some other leads and it turns out that Adam, our driver and connection at Old Camp, will help us out tomorrow.

Aaron was spending endless time in yarn shops helping his Aunt Nancy and Kelly purchase musk ox yarn. I bailed out and went to the grocery store for beer and focaccia for lunch, then rode the bus back to Old Camp Lodge for some peace and quiet with a nap. I got some packing done.

Aaron returned around 1700 (he had to walk the mile back) and we've relaxed together. Showers and an early bedtime are in the forecast this evening. I was able to text back and forth with Diane (she's in Florida visiting relatives) and some friends. Aaron and I are basically stuck here until our flight to Nuuk on Monday morning.

I picked up a reindeer antler outside. It barely fits in my black duffel. I am considering packing other gear around it and taking it home.

Fresh baked Greenlandic bread for breakfast at Old Camp.

Saturday, May 27, 2023 (Aaron)
Kangerlussuaq, Greenland

We had an Old Camp breakfast. They served cereals, fresh-baked breads, cheeses, spreads, many fancy teas, coffee, lots of OJ, and meats.

We rode the 12 DKK ($1.77 USD for both of us total!) bus to the airport. I did some yarn shopping for my aunt and girlfriend. I enjoyed the kang stew. Terry went to the grocery store to save money, then caught the bus back to enjoy bruschetta and drinks for an early dinner.

We weighed ourselves at the airport. I lost 25 pounds during the expedition. Nice weight loss plan.

To ship the gun, I tried the post office, and then Air Greenland freight. They were all closed. That meant I had to haul the 9-pound gun and ammo sling back with a bag full of gifts in 30° temperatures in a 25 MPH gritty headwind back to Old Camp. It was a great treat after the subzero temps on the ice cap. Now, Old Camp was empty except for us. Nice.

I had stashed a pile of breads and spreads from breakfast knowing I wouldn't have the desire to walk back and forth to the airport again. Terry ran out of bread. He did have beers, though. Smart! We committed ourselves to butter sandwiches.

It was a nice zen experience at the lodge.

I did a FaceTime with my Dad and Mom. I paid the roaming fee for cellular in Greenland. It was worth it to me. I showed them around the Old Camp (from WWII), and then shared some vistas and views.

Later... It's 930 p.m. here and I'm sitting at the table alone, as Terry is asleep. This is so neat to have a 10-year celebration of my record-setting South Pole journey, and a 16-year celebration of my first Greenland visit in the same building. I even found some of the old satellite posters I enjoyed from back then.

We had to get up at 530 a.m. tomorrow to eat and catch the airport shuttle for our flight to Nuuk. We arranged it with the lodge staff to make sure we had a place. We're praying for good weather in Nuuk, as Kangerlussuaq has 99% good weather, so we can make our Reykjavik connection the day after.

Sunday, 28 May, 2023 (Terry)
Old Camp Lodge, Kangerlussuaq

I slept pretty well. We have the whole building to ourselves, so it's okay to walk down the hallway to use the toilet without getting dressed.

Breakfast was in another building. It was the same fresh-made bread. We went to the lodge office to arrange shipping the gun and ammo back to Robert. It was $160 to ship, so it wasn't cheap.

I spent the day packing, napping, and eating breakfast bread for lunch, dinner, and snacks. It turns out the supermarket is closed on Sunday and Monday. Monday happens to be a holiday here, so there are few food options.

I listened to a Tim Keller sermon after hearing that he died 9 days ago. "Your plans, God's plans." What a great teacher and Christian man! He will be missed.

We have a flight to Nuuk, Greenland's capital, in the morning. Then, we are on to Iceland for a few days to sightsee, then we head home finally!

How far away Kangerlussuaq, Greenland, is from the rest of the world.

Sunday, May 28, 2023 (Aaron)

It's 930 p.m. here and I'm sitting at the table alone, as Terry is asleep. This is so neat to have a 10-year celebration of my record-setting South Pole journey while at the same time a 16-year celebration of my first Greenland visit in the same building. I even found some of the old satellite posters I enjoyed from back then.

I revelled looking around at the different expedition posters. I found the old weather station poster from when I visited 16 years ago. It's amazing to see things from decades before.

We had to get up at 530 a.m. tomorrow to eat and catch the airport shuttle for our flight to Nuuk. We arranged it with the lodge staff to make sure we had seats. We're praying for good weather in Nuuk, as Kangerlussuaq has 99% good weather, so we can make our Reykjavik connection the day after.

Aaron at Old Camp in the Ulo lodge 2023 (top) and 2008 (bottom).

29 May, 2023 (Terry)

We walked to town for lunch. There were limited choices because it was a national holiday. That's where my symptoms started. I just couldn't eat and headed to the toilet at the restaurant, feeling like was going to faint. Made it through lunch with a to-go box, and then shopped for breakfast food. I walked back to the Nuuk hostel by myself because Aaron wanted to browse around. I laid down and slept the afternoon away.

On Monday we took the morning flight to Nuuk. The hostel we stayed in was in a spectacular location on the water.

Ocean view at our cabin at Inuk Hostel, Nuuk, Greenland.

Monday, May 29, 2023 (Aaron)
Kangerlussuaq, Greenland to Nuuk, Iceland

We awoke, got our gear in place, and went to breakfast at 6 a.m. The female guide from Denmark entertained us with guiding stories for lodge guests. It was her first guiding job. She also was our driver to the airport. We didn't end up having to pay an overweight fee. The staff just checked it in. Good thing I didn't pre-pay or say anything. That saved $200 USD.

We caught our flight to Nuuk. The flight allowed us to see a long stretch of the ice cap from Kangerlussuaq to Nuuk. The view was stunning, to see our long distance unravel before our eyes.

We caught a 10-minute taxi ride ($20 USD) to our lodge on the water. It was a mile out of town, but the views were incredible, right on the Arctic Ocean causeway. The city hotels were far more expensive and had dirty views of the city. This was vastly superior.

We both walked into town after exploring. By then, Terry was having bad stomach troubles. He wouldn't eat hardly anything at the American-styled restaurant we ended up at (the only place open). We did some breakfast grocery shopping, then he walked back while I shopped around town.

I didn't feel I like figuring out the bus, so I walked back. Terry slept most of the day, though we explored the Arctic tide pools. The water was utterly clear.

Sleep!

Tidepools in Nuuk, Greeland.

30 May, 2023 (Terry)

Tuesday Morning, we took the taxi to the airport and caught our delayed flight here (Reykjavik). The Flybys was the best option for the 1-hour drive to Reykjavik. The second bus driver was nice enough to drop us closer to the guest house.

We went out to dinner at a really nice restaurant, but it was wasted on me. I just ate a small bowl of fish chowder and it went down like lead.

Our cozy taxi from the Nuuk airport.

Tuesday, May 30, 2023 (Aaron)
Nuuk, Greenland to Reykjavik, Iceland

We awoke and I fired up a cereal breakfast. Terry was able to eat a little, though he didn't feel good. I felt sorry for him. Hopefully he gets over the stomach bug soon.

We had pre-arranged the taxi with yesterday's driver. He showed up right on time. Our Icelandair flight check-in was odd, as there was no agent until 1.5 hours before the flight. It all worked out, though.

The flight to Reykjavik felt longer than it was. Guess I was tired, knowing there was much traveling to do.

Terry had smartly arranged our bus ride to Reykjavik from the airport ($30 USD total, round trip, for both of us!). The driver "semi-illegally" dropped us much closer to Snorri's guest house so we didn't have to drag our gear a quarter mile. Nice!

We both passed out for a while. I found a fancy Icelandic restaurant and we went. Sadly, Terry struggled badly with food. I ate slowly so I didn't balloon in weight. I knew the Icelandic food wouldn't pack on weight like eating in America.

At night, we arranged an Iceland Golden Circle tour that included all the major sites plus a visit to the Blue Lagoon for $140 USD each. It picked us up from the bus stop down the street.

We both went back and passed out, sleeping through the street traffic in our fourth-floor loft room with a shared bathroom. We had fancy monogrammed bathrobes, towels, and fine toiletries. Super nice!

Aaron's seal skin bed in Nuuk, Greenland.

Wednesday, 31 May, 2023 (Terry)
Snorri's Guest House, Reykjavik

We're staying in a beautiful guesthouse but I'm not able to enjoy it much. I've been sick with gastrointestinal symptoms and marked fatigue since Nuuk, Greenland.

(Later...)

This morning, I was still sick with diarrhea, so I stayed in and slept the day away while Aaron was out exploring.

We have an 11-hour tour booked tomorrow, so I'm counting on turning the corner with the help of medications. I ate some Ramen soup Aaron left with me and had some tea and coffee. I went out for a short walk to see the famous church and Leif Erickson statue.

The famous Hallgrimskirkja church with a statue of Leif Erikson.

Tuesday, May 31, 2023 (Aaron)
Nuuk, Greenland to Reykjavik, Iceland

Terry wasn't feeling well this morning, so I struck out and checked out the shopping district for a bit. There are all the usual tourist shops with trinkets, t-shirts, and the like. But as I explored a bit more, I discovered some cool true Icelandic stores.

At first I wasn't too excited about Iceland but I've warmed up it to pretty quickly. I was too fast to make a judgment based on what other people had said. Definitely need to ignore other people's reviews.

There were a couple of neat knitwear shops, some bigger manufactured and others truly hand-made. The hand-made sweaters were upwards of $600 USD. Ouch! They sure were nice, though.

I checked in with Terry and he wasn't doing too well at all. I went to a quickie mart and bought him some ramen and survival snacks. He had lost a lot of weight and I didn't want him to end up disabled for our big Golden Circle tour tomorrow.

I wanted to eat some tricked-out Icelandic food, so I found a little pub downtown. I enjoyed dried fish, puffin (small pretty bird), and fermented shark. The shark smelled bad but it was pretty good. Classic delicacies. Haha.

Tried to coax Terry out but he was down for the count. Better to rest and feel better for the big tour tomorrow. I went to the Vietnamese Pho place for dinner. Simple and filling and didn't break the bank.

To bed early so we're ready and rested for the Golden Circle Tour and stop at the Blue Lagoon.

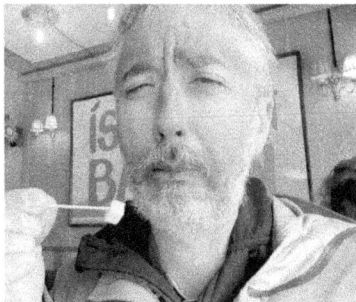

Aaron enjoying fermented shark, an Icelandic delicacy.

Thursday, 1 June, 2023 (Terry)
Snorri's Guesthouse, Reykjavik, Iceland

Glad to feel improved today since we have an all-day tour booked. Appetite is still not back, but I should be okay. After breakfast in the guest house, we headed to bus stop 11 to meet our tour. Elias, our driver and guide, picked us up in a Sprinter van full of other tourists.

The first stop was Thingvellir National Park where parliament meetings were held 1,000 years ago! And, this is where the North American and European tectonic plates meet (and are moving apart at different rates). It's a beautiful area with a large, clear lake and dramatic lava canyons.

Next, we visited the Geysir geothermal area and filmed the Strokkur geyser erupting. We had a light lunch there. Then, we went on to Gullfoss waterfall. It is a massive, impressive waterfall. I tried to photograph it from every viewpoint I could.

Elias stopped at a small farm with Icelandic ponies and a wool shop. Aaron let me use his phone to FaceTime with Diane so she could pick out a hand-knitted shawl for her Iceland souvenir. (~$100). I think she'll enjoy it.

We went on to Kerið Crater Lake. It was formed when a magma chamber collapsed.

The final stop was the Blue Lagoon. We spent more than 2 hours soaking there. Admission included a free drink, mud face mask, and plenty of warm water with people watching. This is a day that Diane would really enjoy.

Back at the room, we dropped off things and walked up to Loki's cafe to have some Icelandic food. I had the rye bread with mashed fish. Very good. Aaron enjoyed his mixed plate.

Thursday, June 1, 2023 (Aaron)
Reykjavik, Iceland

Today was tour day.

We got up early and enjoyed the spectacular European-style breakfast at Snorri's Guest House. The cook had cut up fruit, meats, and cheeses. There were multiple juices, teas, and coffees to drink. I'd never had so many cereal choices with yogurts, types of milk, and other fixings in a guesthouse. Plus, the breads were fresh European-style.

Even though not as fancy as a big chain American hotel (Marriott, etc.) the food selection at Snorri's was far better than anything I've had in America. Having a built-in breakfast is a huge deal. It saves money and, more importantly, time.

We walked to our bus stop. The bus came at the end of our pickup window. We got front seats for the best view, being the last to be picked up.

The tour exited Reykjavik and soon we were exploring the countryside. The guide was funny and knew what'd be interesting. The visits to Thingvellir National Park, Geysir geothermal area, Kerið Crater Lake, and Gullfoss waterfall were excellent. We had enough time to see the sights but not enough time for deep exploration. That was the trade.

We enjoyed lunch at the massive Geysir visitor center. I couldn't believe how big it was. The main attraction geyser shoots off about once every five minutes. It's stunning and rapidly recycles. We didn't have to wait 90 minutes like Old Faithful in Yellowstone. Bonus.

We also had a quick stop at a thermal feature location where we saw people making Icelandic Rye bread in pots buried under piles of sand on the hot geothermal ground. It's called hverabrauð. It takes 24 hours underground (or under dirt with rocks to mark the spot) to cook. The result is super tasty from just rye dough. This wasn't on the official itinerary but it was well appreciated.

The other unofficial stop was at a small farm with friendly Icelandic ponies. They let the group pet them. Maybe they just wanted food. Terry used my phone to FaceTime Diane and bought her a nice handmade Icelandic knit shawl (?). The guide joked that he didn't get a commission stopping here, it was just some people he knew.

Gullfoss Waterfall on Iceland's Golden Circle.

The Blue Lagoon is a great place to unwind after a long expedition.

The unplanned stops were fun. The big stop at the finish was the Blue Lagoon. Though some people complained it was touristy, they're just online whiners. It's touristy because it's awesome. The lagoon is massive, so crowding isn't an issue. I'm glad we got to spend over 2 hours here. Terry and I could've half a day.

We returned to Reykjavik. Terry wasn't feeling good and stayed in the room, living off a bag of pretzels I had gotten. I went out for a bit and brought him back ramen and snacks for his unstable stomach. Went out for some tourist shopping and FaceTime with family back home.

In early June, it's never dark in Reykjavik, not even dusk darkness. The night light level is just a fully overcast day. It made sleeping a bit tough.

A traditional Icelandic dinner of sliced Rye bread with mashed fish (Plokkfiskur), smoked trout, flatbread with smoked lamb, dried fish with butter, and fermented shark at Cafe Loki near Hallgrimskirkja church.

Friday, 2 June, 2023 (Terry)
Snorri's Guest House, Reykjavik, Iceland

It was a relaxing day as we poked around Reykjavik. I left Aaron at the 66° North store spending lots of time picking out an expensive jacket to jog in where he lives now in the northern Rockies.

I shopped for an "Arctic Explorer" hoodie sweater. I finally found one, a great one with "Northern Lights" colors inside the hood. Figure I've earned it.

I had lunch at the Vietnamese restaurant so I could eat some rice and try to help my GI tract back to normal.

I relaxed in the room and did a final packing for the departure tomorrow.

A permanent mailbox for letters to Santa in Reykjavik.

Friday, June 2, 2023 (Aaron)
Reykjavik, Iceland

We enjoyed another excellent Snorri's breakfast. I could do this style of breakfast every day.

Terry wasn't feeling well but braved it out to tour around Reykjavik. I ended up at 66° North and got a great running jacket. I've always wanted one of their pieces since I saw Vilborg Gissurardóttir with the gear in Antarctica. Icelandic outerwear is incredible.

Terry did some wandering around while I was shopping. He didn't pay for cell service in Iceland, so we couldn't reconnect on the street. He texted me from the hotel saying he was staying in because he wasn't feeling well, so I was on my own.

I ate lunch at the Sea Baron and enjoyed the catch of the day I'd never heard of. It was super tasty. Missed having horse meat at another restaurant. I hit up a few Icelandic sweater places. The hand-knit store was great but way out of my price range. I ended up with a few Álafoss Icelandic sweaters. Incredible material.

Later, I connected with Terry. We struck out for the famous Lutheran Icelandic church and ate dinner at Cafe Loki. I had classic Icelandic dried fish, fermented shark, and other Icelandic delicacy food. Terry stomached down soup and bread. He took some meds to try to kill the intestinal bug that's working him over.

Reykjavik is way cooler than I expected. I'd come back here.

Laugavegur Street, the lively tourist shopping street of Reykjavik.

Saturday, 3 June, 2023 (Terry)
Reykjavik, Iceland travel to Salt Lake City, Utah

We were up early to schlep the heavy gear bags several blocks to bus stop 11 for transfer by Flybys (Reykjavik Excursions) to the Keflavik (KEF) airport. All went smoothly, but it was plenty of work with my unwieldy 50-pound black duffel.

I met a nice seat mate on the first leg of the flight, Renee Fitzgerald, who lives near Carlsbad Village! I need to have her over for a glass of wine. She was very interested in our adventure.

We had plenty of time at JFK airport to clear customs, re-check our bags, and relax and eat lots of food in the Delta lounge.

The flight to Salt Lake City was delayed. Aaron got us upgraded to first class, but other than the drinks and food, it was not a comfortable flight. The plane was hot! I was marinating in my own sweat.

At Salt Lake City, we took the shuttle to Fairfield Suites for a shower and collapsed into bed. The jet lag nipped at both of us, so we didn't sleep too well. I was able to change my flight tomorrow to San Diego to an earlier time.

Penthouse accommodations at Snorri's guest house.

Saturday, June 3, 2023 (Aaron)
Reykjavik, Iceland to JFK, New York to Salt Lake City

We begin our long haul home. We had to be out before break-fast, so we asked the guesthouse cook to prepare a classic European breakfast and put it into our room's mini-fridge. She delivered. It was all great. Terry seemed better, though still struggling.

The haul of multiple 50-pound bags a quarter mile to the bus stop was a slog. Terry's pre-arranged bus service got us right to the airport. I ate my last salmon wrap meal at the airport. Super tasty. Blows away American offerings. It was better than stuff I've had in many restau-rants. European food is so much better than American.

Terry survived on the bag of remaining bag pretzels I gave him. He seems to be in survival-eating mode. Hope he's better soon.

We caught our flight and headed to JFK. The airplane food from the Iceland side in Comfort+ was great. The short ribs were super tender. Terry struggled but finished his off. My airline status paid off, giving us $800 in upgraded seats. Sweet.

5 hours later...

JFK is where Terry came to life. His appetite returned with a ven-geance. He ate at least two or three plates of food in the Delta Lounge. Glad he recovered. I refrained from overeating. I didn't want to gain back the 25 pounds I lost on the expedition.

Soon, we were on our way to Salt Lake City. It was a long nearly 5-hour flight. Being in first class didn't hurt. Platinum Medallion status upgrades had its privileges. Terry enjoyed it. He said, "I need to travel with you more often, Aaron." Not sure if he'd ever flown first class be-fore? It was a great way to end our travels together.

We overnighted in a Salt Lake City Marriott-brand hotel. We got Uber Eats dinner from Black Bear Diner. Terry seemed glad for the comfort food.

Sunday, 4 June, 2023 (Terry)
Salt Lake City to San Diego flight

We went to the airport and checked those heavy bags for the last time. We then went to the Delta lounge for a second breakfast.

I saw Aaron off, then it was smooth sailing to San Diego where Diane picked me up at the airport. We encountered the usual heavy Sunday afternoon traffic in North County, making it frustrating to get home.

Our shaggy puppies were happy to see me. It's as if I was never gone now.

I was going to put off chores, but the backyard was such a mess that Diane wouldn't even take the dogs out there. So, I mowed and raked and repeated, then showered and relaxed for the evening.

Now I'm back to normal life. I need to unpack, get caught up, and write a book about our adventure!

Strokkur geyser on Iceland's Golden Circle delivers eruptions every few minutes.

Sunday, June 4, 2023 (Aaron)
Salt Lake City, Utah

We caught our shuttle to the airport.

The check-in agent gave Terry a hard time, trying to tack on a huge oversize fee to his bag. I should have had him go with me to the premium agents. My bags were just as big. I despise when agents do that, picking and choosing. Terry said this was the last leg of a massive trip. The dude had the gall to say, "Well, I'll let it pass but I'll put a note in your account." Very disappointing. You never know who you'll get.

We spent our last two hours together in the Delta lounge eating. We didn't talk too much, other than what we'd do working on books like this one. Terry had switched his flight to San Diego to earlier in the day so he didn't have to suffer bad San Diego North County afternoon traffic.

We parted ways and I was on my flight.

It was an uneventful flight home. I had Kelly pick me up and I was right back in regular life again.

It was an excellent expedition with Terry Williams, M.D., the best expedition partner ever!

Terry started at 120 lbs and dropped to 105 lbs. He has gained it all back. I lost 25 pounds and gained back 5 pounds by mid-August 2023.

Breakfast at Snorri's Guest House in Reykjavik is a feast every morning.

Unexpected Development

(Written by Aaron)

Shortly after returning from the expedition, I traveled to San Diego to visit friends and family in mid-June. I met up with Terry. We recounted our expedition trials and successes. The reunion was fun, as Terry and his wife Diane invited my family and girlfriend over for lunch. Everyone got to meet everyone.

All was going well over the next month. Terry had begun in earnest on this book. He wanted to share the experience and his and my faith with as many people as possible.

"I want to get the story out," Terry said.

This was Terry's biggest expedition ever. He planned to write this book you are reading now. Crossing Greenland was one of my biggest expeditions. I'd worked toward it for 16 years. Both of us were looking forward to a long and productive friendship.

Then, on July 16, I received a shocking text message from Diane.

Sun, Jul 16 at 16:17

Hi Aaron. I wanted to make you aware of the path we've been on the last few days and ask you for prayer. Terry is in a Kaiser hospital in San Diego. He has a brain tumor. He was taken in for a needle biopsy this morning. We will have results back in 4-5 days. Our friends from church have been taking good care of us, from the very beginning. God provided our dear friend Matt from our Life Group at church, an ER doc at Palomar Health, to be on duty when we were sent there from Kaiser urgent care on Friday morning. When he saw the CT scan results he let his wife, Lorraine know so she could come and be with us. We are blessed, know God is in complete control, and are taking one day at a time, not looking ahead to worst case scenarios. Love to you and Kelly

Terry had brain cancer.

As soon as the doctors delivered the initial diagnosis, Terry's life changed. The initial prognosis was that he likely only had a few months to live. The glioblastoma cancer that he had was highly aggressive. And, worst of all, it was in the late stages. This type of cancer was one of the worst possible to develop.

Terry said that the cancer was not likely even present when we were on our expedition. Being a doctor, he was well-versed in what was going on, the timeline, and everything else involved. I just couldn't believe Terry was hit by this kind of blow.

As soon as I found out, I bought a ticket to fly to San Diego to visit Terry, knowing his time was short. He and I worked together so I could type up Terry's journals. Terry had already made good progress on the book. He had the most important thing I couldn't come up with—his biography and perspective on his experience.

Terry had made incredible progress right up to his tragic diagnosis. I took over the book, knowing how important it was to Terry to get this story out.

Undertaking an unsupported expedition for two men in midlife and later in life is rare. The effort and time required to succeed is substantial. Not many older people pursue polar exploration due to the long and endless hours involved. The physical work is often difficult to comprehend.

Terry Williams delivered a command performance in his epic crossing of the Greenland ice cap along the Arctic Circle.

Glossary

Food forward bag

A bag of food that wasn't eaten but is kept for later days when food is short.

Fur ruff

A natural fur border sewn on the leading edge of our working parka hoods. The purpose is much more than fashion. The ruff, usually of wolverine fur (Aaron's is a combination of wolverine and beaver), creates a warm microenvironment around your face to protect it from cold wind that can cause frostbite in minutes, and to blunt the wind noise.

Pogies

Insulated overmittens designed to be attached to the top of ski poles. Skiers insert their hands into the pogies with gloves to add an extra layer of hand warmth.

Pulk

A plastic sled loaded with our gear, fuel, and food to sustain us on the crossing.

Sastrugi

A formation on the snow surface shaped by the wind, anywhere from a few inches to a few feet high. Their surface is hard, which is welcome, but these form an obstacle to get past that can stop the skier or more particularly the heavy sled we are towing. We each developed our own style to get past them. Aaron tended to muscle the sled over. I used momentum to try to keep the sled moving.

Ski shift

We divided our ski day into shifts of 75 minutes, followed by a break of 15 minutes when we drank, ate a bar or other snack, drank some more, emptied bladders and made any needed clothing adjustments. For the sake of efficiency, we tried to avoid other unscheduled stops, but they were sometimes unavoidable if one of us had to adjust clothing or urinate. With 6 ski shifts a day plus breaks and a "bonus shift" of 30 minutes, we were out skiing for 9 hours 30 minutes each day.

Trail harden

Get strong on the trail...

Unconsolidated snow

Loose snow that has no structure and blows around.

Wind deposited snow

Loose, soft snow left between wind slabs or sastrugi, particularly on the leeward side of one of the imperceptible terrain features we were navigating. We came to despise these sections which required so much energy to tow the heavy pulks through.

Wind slab

A place where the wind has scoured away any overlying loose snow and left a flat surface that is usually ideal to pull a sled across.

Expedition Route Map and Profile

Route: Ice cap near Isortoq to Hill 660 near Kangerlussuaq
Total GPS daily measured miles: 309.4 miles (497.9 km)
Actual miles: ~320 miles (515 km)

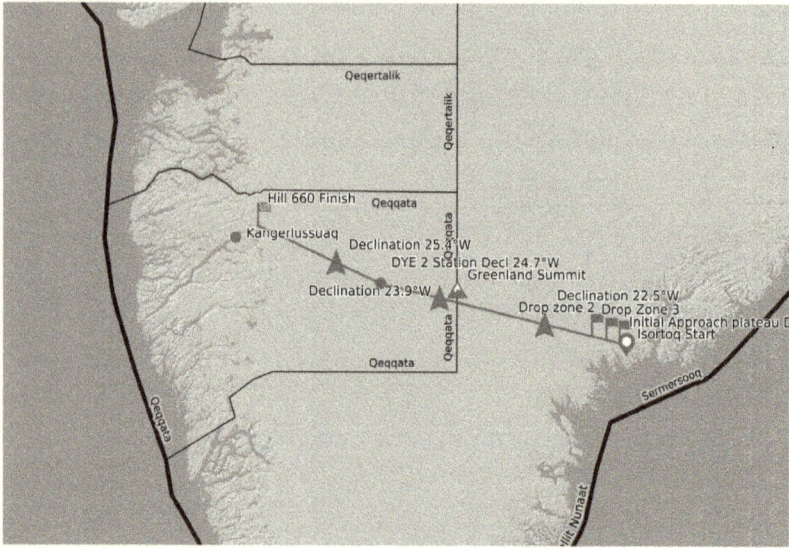

Expedition Route map
WGS84
UTM

| 125 | 250 | 375 | 500 | 625 km |

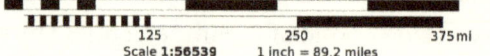

| 125 | 250 | 375 mi |

Scale **1:56539**   1 inch = 89.2 miles

MN
-23.7°

Elevation Profile

Greenland Expedition Route
range 1322' to 8182' gain 8337' loss 7999' exaggeration 101.7x

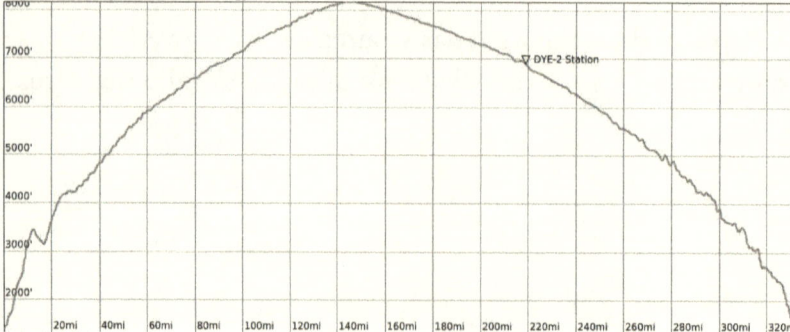

Isortoq   Hill 660

Author's Note

I hope you enjoyed this book. Please consider giving it a 5-star rating and add a few words about your reading experience at your favorite online retailer.

The link below with a QR code will take you to the book's web page. From there, you can follow links to various online retailers.

Giving my book 5-stars and a short written review about why you enjoyed it will help me immensely.

Thank you!

Terry Williams

www.sastrugipress.com/books/two-friends-and-a-polar-bear/

Use your smart device to scan the QR code for the book's webpage.

About the Authors

Terry Williams, MD

is the father of four and grandfather of ten, retired from a 32-year practice of Emergency Medicine in California. He is the author of several medical papers and Emergency Medicine textbook chapters. In addition to his full-time medical work in California, he has treated patients in Guatemala, Saudi Arabia, on cruise ships around the world, in Northern India, Thailand, and the highlands of Papua New Guinea. He is also a whitewater kayaker and climber with summits of Sierra 14ers, several of the Cascade volcanoes, and two of the Seven Summits (Aconcagua and Kilimanjaro).

He has served as an expedition doctor on climbs, whitewater runs, and in wilderness/primitive settings. He has served on the board of an international missions/humanitarian organization, Global Fellowship, and now resides in northern San Diego County with his wife of 48 years. He also serves as a medical team manager on San Diego's Urban Search and Rescue (USAR) Team, California Task Force 8.

Aaron Linsdau

is the second-only American to ski alone from the coast of Antarctica to the South Pole, setting a world record for surviving the longest expedition ever for that trip. He has walked across Yellowstone National Park in winter, crossed the Greenland Tundra alone, trekked through the Sahara Desert, attempted to climb Denali solo, and successfully climbed Mt. Kilimanjaro.

Aaron is an Eagle Scout and has received the Outstanding Eagle Scout Award. He holds a bachelor's degree in electrical engineering and a master's degree in computational science. Aaron wrote the book and produced the film *Antarctic Tears* and the show *World Beyond*. Aaron has written 37 books including the guidebooks for the 2017 and 2024 total solar eclipses.

He is an expert at building resilience to overcome adversity. He is a motivational speaker on adversity, risk, and safety. His methods for overcoming challenges, using his stories and experiences, entertain thousands. Book him at his website: www.aaronlinsdau.com.

Visit Aaron's YouTube channel: www.youtube.com/@alinsdau or scan the QR Code:

Books by the authors

50 Jackson Hole Photography Hotspots

This guide reveals the best Jackson Hole photography spots. Learn what locals and insiders know to find the most impressive and iconic photography locations in the United States. This is an excellent companion guide to the *Jackson Hole Hiking Guide.*

www.sastrugipress.com/books/50-jackson-hole-photography-hotspots/

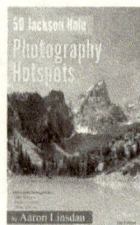

Adventure Expedition One
by Aaron Linsdau M.S. & Terry Williams, M.D.

Create, finance, enjoy, and return safely from your first expedition. Learn the techniques explorers use to achieve their goals and have a good time doing it. Acquire the skills, find the equipment, and learn the planning necessary to pull off an expedition.

www.sastrugipress.com/books/adventure-expedition-one/

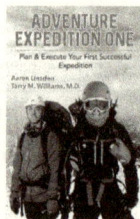

Antarctic Tears

Experience the honest story of solo polar exploration. This inspirational true book will make readers both cheer and cry. Coughing up blood and fighting skin-freezing temperatures were only a few of the perils Aaron Linsdau faced. Travel with him on a world-record expedition to the South Pole.

www.sastrugipress.com/books/antarctic-tears/

How to Keep Your Feet Warm in the Cold

Keep your feet warm in cold conditions on chilly adventures with techniques described in this book. Packed with dozens and dozens of ideas, learn how to avoid having cold feet ever again in your outdoor pursuits

www.sastrugipress.com/books/how-to-keep-your-feet-warm-in-the-cold/

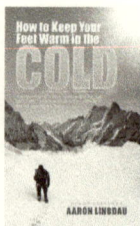

Lost at Windy Corner

Windy Corner on Denali has claimed fingers, toes, and even lives. What would make someone brave lethal weather, crevasses, and avalanches to attempt to summit North America's highest mountain? Aaron Linsdau shares the experience of climbing Denali alone and how you can apply the lessons to your life.

www.sastrugipress.com/books/lost-windy-corner/

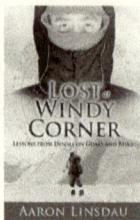

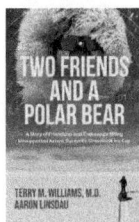

About the Author

Aaron Linsdau is the second-only American to ski alone from the coast of Antarctica to the South Pole (730 miles / 1174 km). He set the world record for surviving the longest expedition ever for the Hercules Inlet to the South Pole route.

Aaron Linsdau at the South Pole.

Visit Aaron's YouTube channel: www.youtube.com/@alinsdau or scan the QR Code:

www.ingramcontent.com/pod-product-compliance
Lightning Source LLC
Chambersburg PA
CBHW032100080426
42733CB00006B/352